Bayonet Training for Allied Armies in the First World War

Bayonet Training for Allied Armies in the First World War

Four Manuals for Infantry Soldiers of the Early 20th Century

ILLUSTRATED

Bayonet Training
William H. Waldron

and

Three Bayonet Training Manuals

LEONAUR

Bayonet Training for Allied Armies in the First World War
Four Manuals for Infantry Soldiers of the Early 20th Century
Bayonet Training
By William H. Waldron
and
Three Bayonet Training Manuals

ILLUSTRATED

FIRST EDITION

Leonaur is an imprint of Oakpast Ltd

Copyright in this form © 2022 Oakpast Ltd

ISBN: 978-1-915234-10-0 (hardcover)
ISBN: 978-1-915234-11-7 (softcover)

http://www.leonaur.com

Publisher's Notes

Contents

Notes on Bayonet Training

Adapted from a Canadian Publication

War Department,
Washington, August 16, 1917.
The following pamphlet, Notes on Bayonet Training, No. 2, published for the information of all concerned. (300.6, A. G. O.)

By Order of the Secretary of War:

H. L. Scott,
Major General, Chief of Staff.

Official:

H. P. McCain,
The Adjutant General.

PART 1

Introduction

PHYSICAL FITNESS.

It has been proved that one of the most important factors in this war is physical fitness and development of the fighting spirit. Courage is only developed in a man by his being trained to have the greatest confidence in his fighting weapon. It is just as absurd to send a man forward to fight with a bayonet without having complete confidence in his weapon, as it would be to put an untrained man in the ring against a professional prize fighter. The lack of confidence on the part of the untrained man would be about the same in both cases.

FINAL ASSAULT PRACTICE.

Officers and non-commissioned officers must themselves become good fighters if they are to teach others how to fight, and their success as leaders depends to a very large extent upon their ability as instructors.

Looking at the question broadly it may be stated that the aim of training is the improvement of the fighting quality of a mass, and those who are least efficient should receive the most attention so as to bring them up to the plane of their comrades, as each man in the mass depends upon his confidence in himself and in his comrades as fighters.

Bayonet fighting must be taught as boxing, fencing, and wrestling are taught—by actual contact and not merely theoretically. To tell a man how to box and give him instructions by the hour will never make him a boxer. He must combine theory with practice. He must put on the gloves and measure his skill against that of others, and the more he does this, provided he is instructed on the right lines, the greater degree of proficiency to which he will attain. From a fighting point of view, boxing is most invaluable as an aid to training.

STIMULUS OF PHYSICAL CONTACT.

The aim is to develop the soldier of every rank into an ideal fighting man, and it may be put bluntly that progress in training is frequently hindered by the failure of the recruit to apply the natural fighting spirit. It is here where "in-fighting disarming practice," for instance, is such a valuable adjunct to training. The soldier's fighting spirit must be drawn out by actual physical contact.

Regimental officers should be more proficient in the use of the fighting weapons than their men, because the fact of the men knowing that their officers are capable fighters creates a feeling of confidence.

THE SPIRIT OF THE BAYONET.

Uniformity in training is also an important point, as men going into action are buoyed up by the fact that their comrades on their right and left are capable of doing their share at the critical moment.

All ranks must understand that the enemy method of bayonet fighting is not the same as our method. Therefore, the greatest control of the rifle and bayonet is necessary in order to meet any form of attack.

The spirit of the bayonet must be inculcated into all ranks so that they go forward with that aggressive determination and confidence of superiority born of continual practice, without which a bayonet assault will not be effective.

Notes

(1) All "in-fighting" practices can be done with parrying poles padded at the ends representing rifle and bayonet, or with equipment, *viz*, spring muskets, gloves, masks, and body pads.

(2) Any low point may be effectively parried with the butt, and after parrying the butt can be used to disable opponent.

(3) The first object after parrying point with hand or arm is to disable opponent. Secondly, to disarm and kill.

(4) Troops armed with bayonet only can be effectively taught to repel attack against rifle and bayonet.

(5) Any simple method of Ju-jitsu, wrestling, and boxing should be taught and encouraged.

Series "A"-1-8

LONG POINT, SHORT POINT, AND JAB.

Reference, Paragraphs 19 to 30, Notes on Bayonet Training, March, 1917.

Each dummy must be regarded as an actual armed opponent, and each line of dummies as an enemy line—attacking, defending, or retiring—and be disposed of accordingly.

1. On guard.
2. Assault practice—On guard.
3. Long point, at dummy on ground.
4. Foot on dummy, left hand up, vigorous withdrawal.
5. Short point—Position.
6. Short point at dummy, advancing rear foot.
7. Right hand up, withdrawal ready for jab.
8. Jab—Advancing rear foot. Withdraw, passing through dummies at on guard position.

SERIES "A."—1.   ON GUARD.

SERIES "A."—2.   ASSAULT PRACTICE—ON GUARD.

SERIES "A."—3.   LONG POINT. AT DUMMY ON GROUND.

SERIES "A."—4.   FOOT ON DUMMY, LEFT HAND UP, VIGOROUS WITHDRAWAL.

SERIES "A."—5.   SHORT POINT, POSITION.

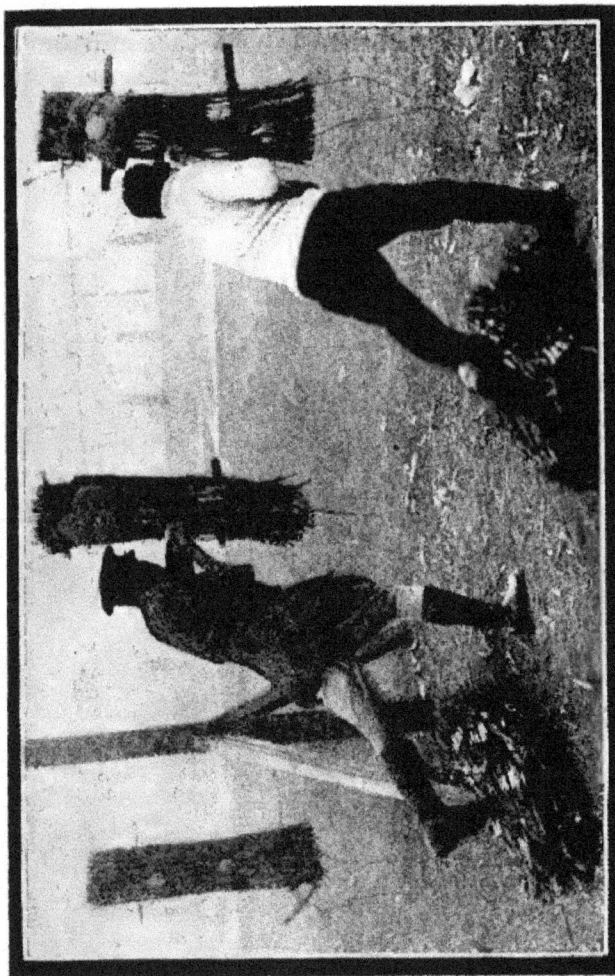

SERIES "A."—G.   SHORT POINT AT DUMMY, ADVANCING REAR FOOT.

SERIES "A."—7.   RIGHT HAND UP, WITHDRAWAL READY FOR JAB.

JAB, ADVANCING REAR FOOT, WITHDRAW, PASSING THROUGH DUMMIES AT ON GUARD POSITION.

SERIES "A."—8.

Series "B"–9–14

ASSAULT PRACTICE.

Reference, Paragraphs 41 to 55, Notes on Bayonet Training, March, 1917.

9. Charging at high port. The threatening, yet defensive, "On Guard" position will be assumed at least 10 yards from the enemy.

10. Jumping from parapet, with point on dummy.

11. Control and direction of point.

12. Point leading on landing.

13. Foot on dummy, left hand up, vigorous withdrawal.

14. On guard and forward.

CHARGING AT HIGH PORT.

SERIES " B."—9.

SERIES "B."—10.   JUMPING FROM PARAPET, WITH POINT ON DUMMY.

SERIES "B."—11.　　　　CONTROL AND DIRECTION OF POINT.

POINT LEADING ON LANDING.

SERIES "B."—12.

SERIES "B."—13.   FOOT ON DUMMY. LEFT HAND UP. VIGOROUS WITHDRAWAL.

SERIES "B."—14.

ON GUARD AND FORWARD.

Series "C"-15-20

DIRECTION PRACTICE AT THRUSTING RING.

15. On guard.
16. Long point.
17. Short point—position.
18. Short point.
19. Jab position.
20. Jab.

ON GUARD.

SERIES "C." 15.

SERIES "C."—16.   LONG POINT.

SHORT POINT.

SERIES "C."—18.

SHORT POINT—POSITION.

SERIES "C."—19.

JAB POSITION.

SERIES "C."—20.

JAB.

Series "D"-21-24

DEMONSTRATION OF SUCCESSFUL ATTACK, SHOWING METHOD
OF WITHDRAWING THE RIFLE FROM VICTIM.

21. Successful point: victim seizing rifle.
22. Victim forced to ground.
23. Strong withdrawal.
24. Ready for further action with short point.

SERIES: "D."—21.   SUCCESSFUL POINT: VICTIM SEIZING RIFLE.

SERIES "D."—22.

VICTIM FORCED TO GROUND.

STRONG WITHDRAWAL.

SERIES " D."—23.

Series "E"–25–30

Use of Butt.

Reference, Paragraphs 31 to 36, Notes on Bayonet Training, March, 1917.

25. Right parry.
26. Attack continued with butt to flank.
27. Points forced up after parry.
28. Butt to fork.
29. Left low parry.
30. Butt to head.

RIGHT PARRY.

SERIES "E."—25.

SERIES "E."—26.   ATTACK CONTINUED WITH BUTT TO FLANK.

SERIES "E."—27.

POINTS FORCED UP AFTER PARRY.

SERIES "E."—28.   BUTT TO FORK.

LEFT LOW PARRY.

SERIES "I."—49.   ADVANCE, STRIKING OPPONENT'S LEFT HAND FROM RIFLE.

Series "F" 31-33

FINAL ASSAULT.

Reference, Paragraphs 41 to 55, Notes on Bayonet Training, March, 1917.

31. Final assault.
32. Final assault.
33. Final assault.

SERIES "F."—31. FINAL ASSAULT (1).

FINAL ASSAULT (2).

SERIES "F."—32.

SERIES "F."—33.

FINAL ASSAULT (3).

Series "G"-34-41

"IN-FIGHTING."

Parry point outward with left hand. Step in, seizing opponent's left wrist firmly with the right hand. Grip rifle with left hand (back of hand down). Swing rifle upward and to the right, at the same time stepping in, bringing left knee violently to fork. Disarm, using butt or point.

34. Parry point outward with left hand.

35. Step in, seizing opponent's left wrist firmly with right hand.

36. Grip the rifle with left hand, back of the hand down.

37. Swing the rifle upward and to the right, at the same time stepping in, retaining grasp on opponent's left wrist.

38. Left knee, violently to fork.

39. Force opponent to ground, and disarm.

40. Use butt or point.

41. Using point to kill.

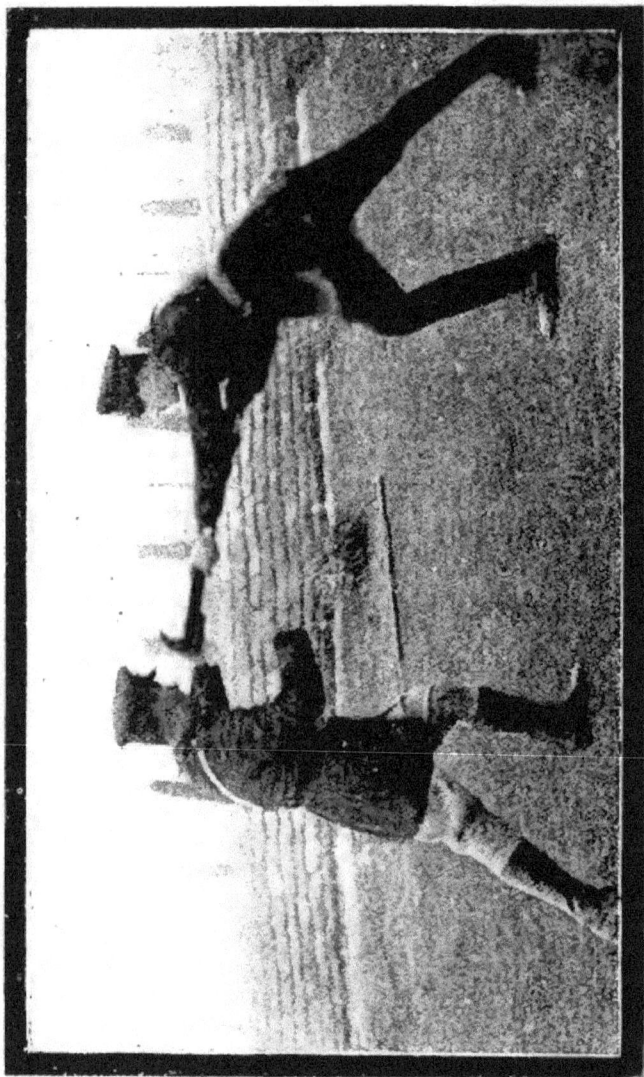

SERIES "G."—34.   PARRY POINT OUTWARD WITH LEFT HAND.

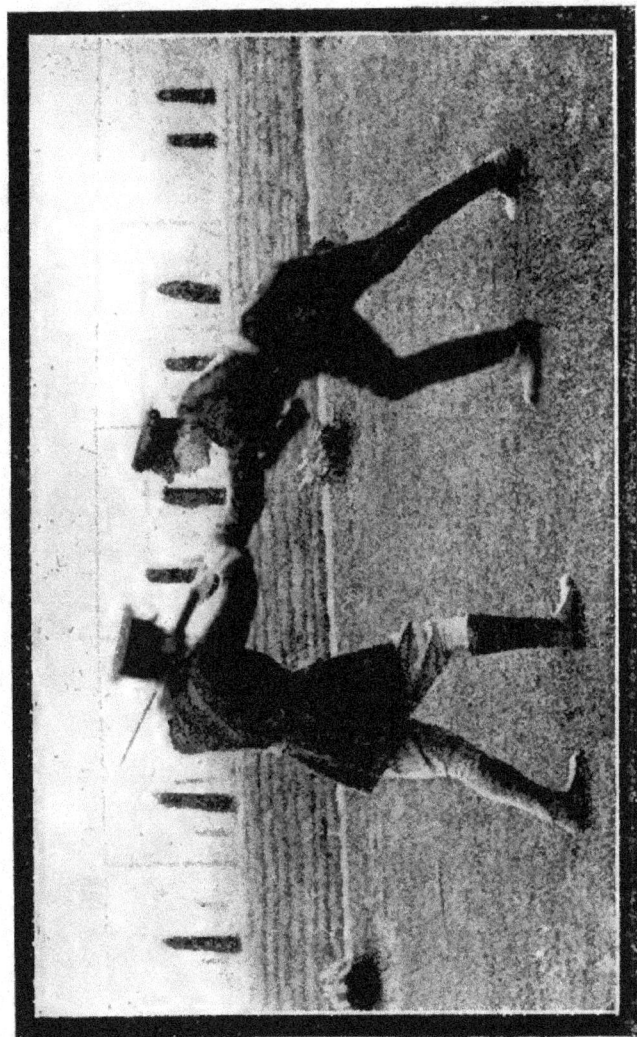

STEP IN, SEIZING OPPONENT'S LEFT WRIST FIRMLY WITH RIGHT HAND.

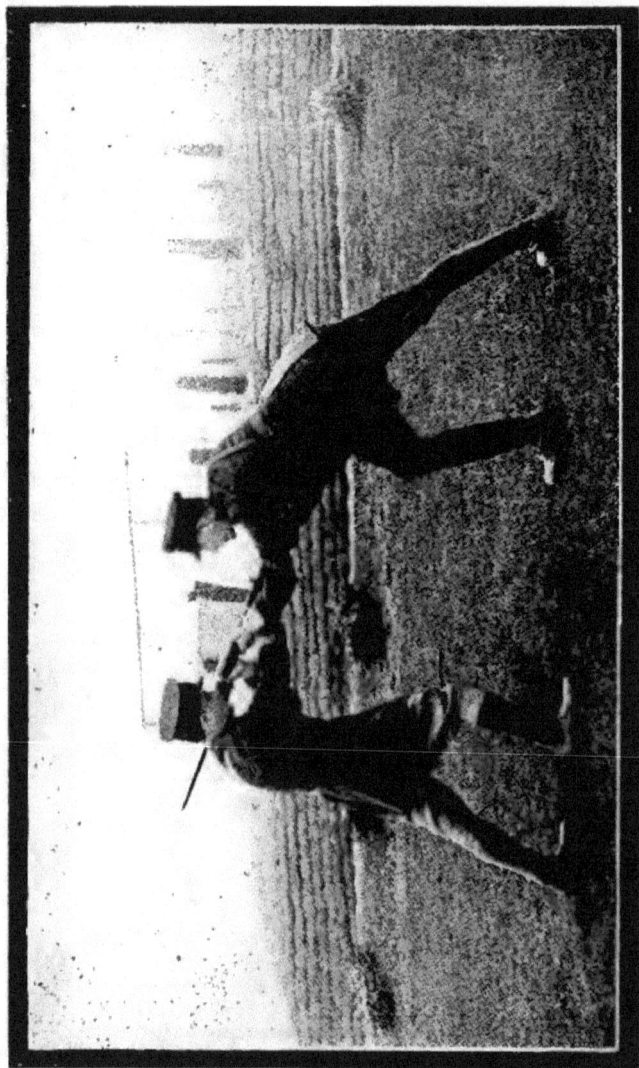

SERIES "G."—36.   GRIP THE RIFLE WITH LEFT HAND, BACK OF THE HAND DOWN.

SWING THE RIFLE UPWARD AND TO THE RIGHT, AT THE SAME TIME STEPPING IN, RETAINING GRASP ON OPPONENT'S LEFT WRIST.

SERIES "G." —37.

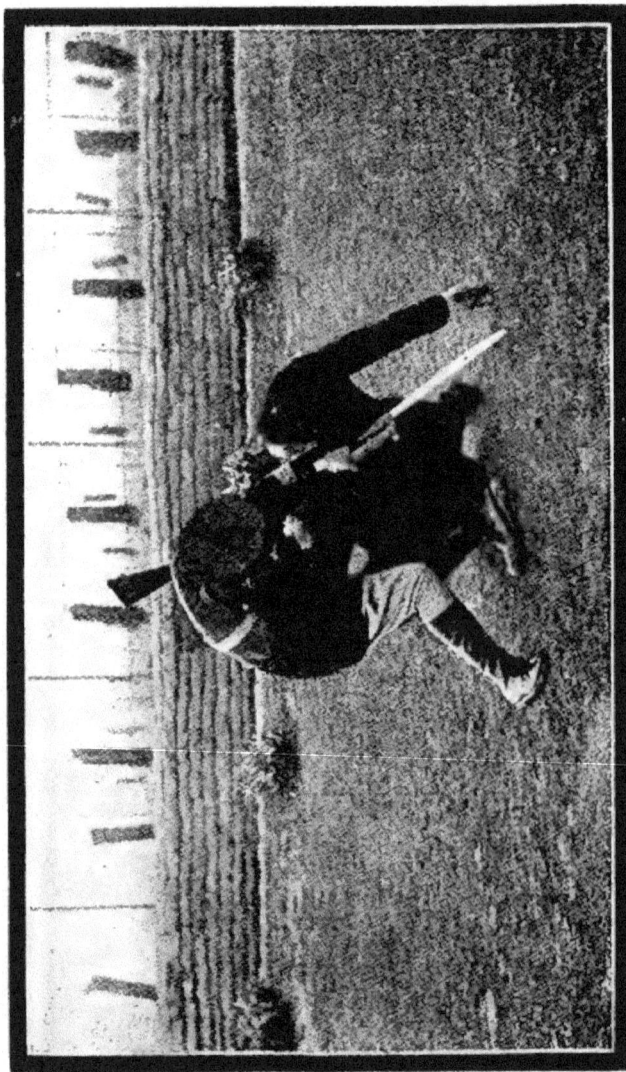

SERIES "G."—38. LEFT KNEE, VIOLENTLY TO FORK.

SERIES "G."—39.   FORCE OPPONENT TO GROUND, AND DISARM.

SERIES "G."—40.   USE BUTT OR POINT.

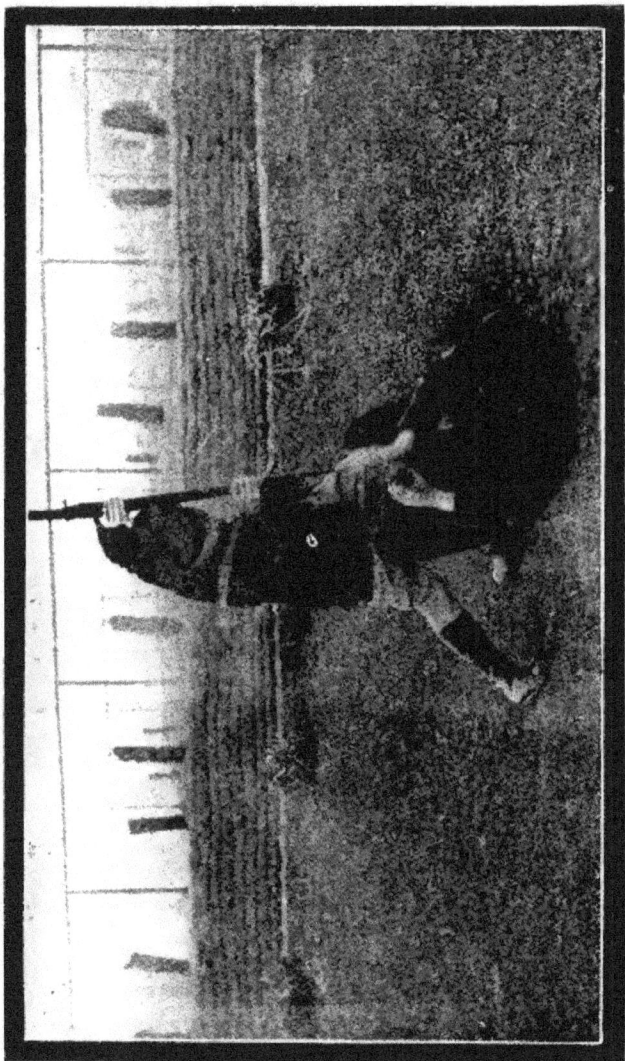

SERIES "G."—41.

USING POINT TO KILL.

Series "H"-42-47

"In-Fighting."

Parry point outward with right hand, kicking at fork or shin with rear foot and gripping rifle with right hand (back of hand down), swing rifle upward and to the left. Force point to ground, at the same time stepping in, vigorously charging or tripping opponent. Disarm and kill.

42. Parry point outward with right hand.
43. Kicking at fork or shin with rear foot, and gripping rifle with right hand, back of hand down.
44. Swing rifle upward and to the left.
45. Force point to ground, stepping in.
46. Vigorously charging or tripping.
47. Disarm and kill.

PARRY POINT OUTWARD WITH RIGHT HAND.

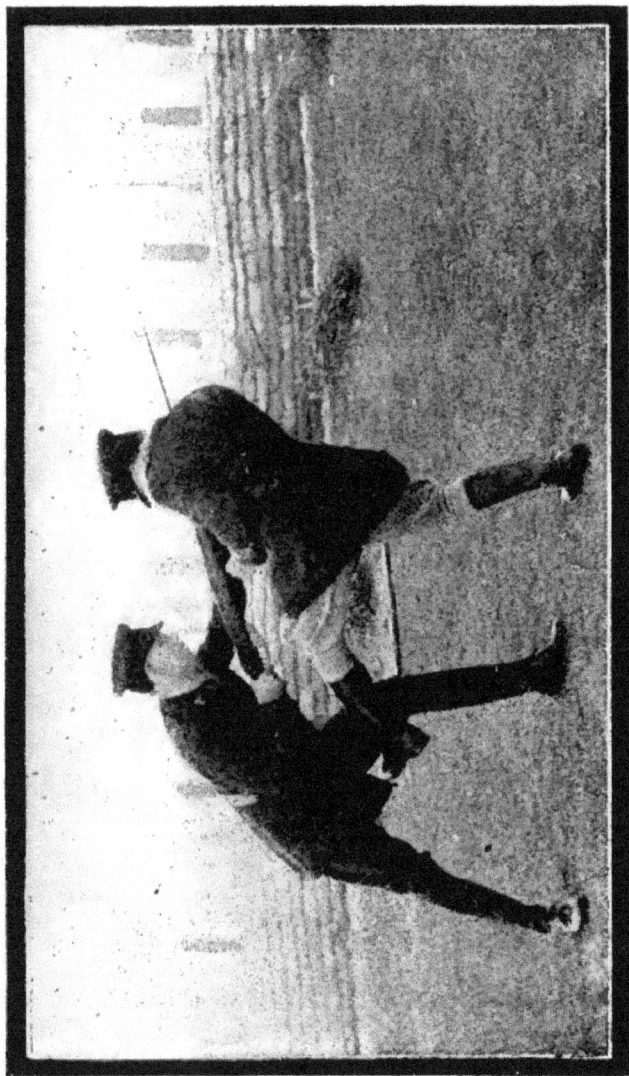

KICKING AT FORK OR SHIN WITH REAR FOOT, AND GRIPPING RIFLE WITH RIGHT HAND, BACK OF HAND DOWN.

Series "II."—43.

SWING RIFLE UPWARD AND TO THE LEFT.

FORCE POINT TO GROUND, STEPPING IN.

VIGOROUSLY CHARGING OR TRIPPING.

DISARM AND KILL.

Series "J"-48-53

"In-Fighting."

Parry point outward and grasp rifle with right hand. Step in, striking opponent's left hand from rifle with left hand, and swing left elbow violently to jaw, disarming opponent, using butt to head and killing with point.

48. Parry with hand.
49. Advance, striking opponent's left hand from rifle.
50. Left elbow to jaw.
51. Attack successful, opponent disarmed.
52. Butt to head.
53; Kill with point.

PARRY WITH HAND.

SERIES "J."—48.

SERIES "J."—49.   ADVANCE, STRIKING OPPONENT'S LEFT HAND FROM RIFLE.

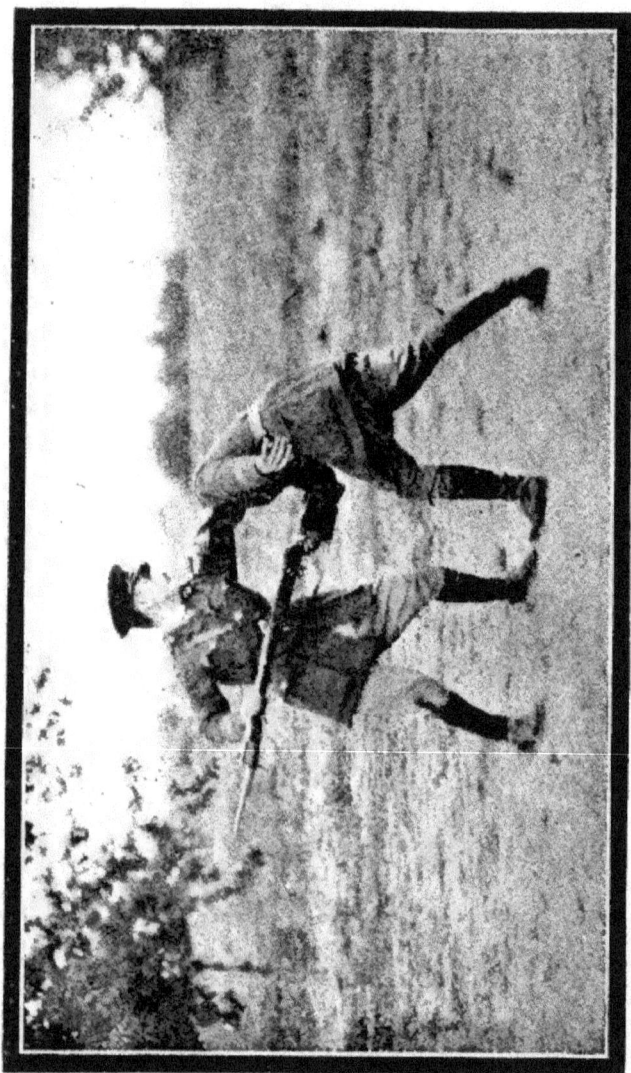

SERIES "J."—50.   LEFT ELBOW TO JAW.

SERIES "J."—51.   ATTACK SUCCESSFUL, OPPONENT DISARMED.

SERIES "J."—49.   ADVANCE, STRIKING OPPONENT'S LEFT HAND FROM RIFLE.

SERIES "J."—53.

KILL, WITH POINT.

Series "K"–54–57

METHOD OF USING RIFLE AT CLOSE QUARTERS.

54. Attack.
55. Parried and points forced to ground.
56. Contact results.
57. Disengagement to jabbing position.

SERIES "K."—54.

ATTACK.

SERIES "K."—55.   PARRIED AND POINTS FORCED TO GROUND.

SERIES "K."—56.

CONTACT RESULTS.

SERIES "K."—57. DISENGAGEMENT TO JABBING POSITION.

Series "L"–58–59

METHOD OF USING KNIFE (CARRIED IN PUTTEE) IN CONJUNCTION WITH THE RIFLE AND BAYONET AT CLOSE QUARTERS.

58. Reaching for knife in contact after parried attack.
59. Stab at groin.

SERIES "L."—58.   REACHING FOR KNIFE IN CONTACT AFTER PARRIED ATTACK.

STAB AT GROIN.

Series "M"-60-61

METHODS OF DISENGAGING AND FEINTING.

60. Advance to attack.
61. Disengagement low on parry and dashing in with point.

ADVANCE TO ATTACK.

DISENGAGEMENT LOW ON PARRY AND DASHING IN WITH POINT.

SERIES "M."—61.

Series "N"-62

A Method of Meeting Attacks.

62. Duck and low point.

DUCK AND LOW POINT.

SERIES "N."—62.

Bayonet Training Manual

Prepared at the School of Arms Fort Sill, Okla.

War Department.
Document No. 754.
Office of the Adjutant General.

War Department,
Washington, February 26, 1918.
The following "Bayonet Training Manual," prepared at the School of Arms, Fort Sill, Okla., is approved and published for the information and guidance of the Armies of the United States.
(062.1 A. G. O.)
By order of the Secretary of War,

John Biddle.
Major General, Acting Chief of Staff.
Official:
H. P. McCain.
The Adjutant General.

U. S. Bayonet Manual, 1918

Section 1

Introductory

The Spirit of the Bayonet.

1. It is an easy matter to teach the few simple technical details of bayonet combat, but an instructor's success will be measured by his ability to instil into his men the will and desire to use the bayonet. This spirit is infinitely more than the physical efforts displayed on our athletic fields; more than the enthusiasm of the prize-ring; more, even, than the grim determination of the firing line—it is an intense eagerness to fight and kill hand to hand, and is the overwhelming impulse behind every successful bayonet assault.

Bayonet fighting is possible only because every red-blooded man naturally possesses the fighting instinct. This inherent desire to fight and kill must be carefully watched for and encouraged by the instructor. It first appears in a recruit when he begins to handle his bayonet with facility, and increases as his confidence grows. With the mastering of his weapon there comes to him a sense of personal fighting superiority and a desire for physical conflict. He knows that he can fight and win. His practice becomes snappy and full of strength. He longs to test his ability against an enemy's body; to prove that his bayonet is irresistible. He pictures an enemy at every practice thrust and drives home his bayonet with strength, precision and satisfaction. Such a man will fight as he has trained—consistently, spiritedly, and effectively. While waiting for the zero hour he will not fidget nervously. He will go over the top and win.

Successful training implies that men will use on the battlefield what they have learned on the drill-ground. To do this a man must move to the attack possessed not only of a determination to win, but also of a perfect confidence in his third arm—the rifle. Such a confidence is born only of long, constant practice, which is the very essence of bayonet training.

Without this, a bayonet assault will fail. The man who bores in at a dead run enjoys the advantage of a superior morale. The man who waits to fence loses his own nerve and helps the enemy take heart. The enemy may have a longer weapon than ours. This gives him the advantage if we stand off and fence, but gives us the advantage if we close with him.

The growth of the spirit of the bayonet is fostered by short talks on what has already been accomplished with the bayonet. The men must be thoroughly informed of probable treachery on the part of the enemy. They must be informed of the possible enemy tricks of pretending to surrender or to be wounded, only to fire upon or bayonet their prospective captors the instant they lessen their aggressiveness.

The bayonet is the deciding factor in every assault, and the soldier must realise that its successful employment requires of him not only individual physical courage, but also perfect discipline and a thorough knowledge of teamwork. In a bayonet fight the nerviest, best disciplined and most skilful man wins—the will to use the bayonet plus cold steel and thorough training assure success.

CONTINUOUS TRAINING.

2. The perfect confidence of the soldier in his weapon as required by this manual is the outcome only of long, continuous practice. To this end bayonet training will be kept up at all times except while actually in the trenches.

DEVELOPMENT OF THE INDIVIDUAL.

3. It is absolutely essential that each man be taught to think and act for himself, and there must be no interval of time between the thinking and the acting. To attain this end, make the men use their brains and eyes to the fullest extent (by carrying out the practices, so far as possible, without words of command, i.e., by demonstration. Cause them to parry sticks, to thrust at a shifting target as soon as it is stationary, etc. The class should always work in pairs and act on the principle of "master and pupil" alternately. This in itself tends to develop individuality and confidence. Sharp, jerky words of command produce mechanical movements of the piece and will not be used.

Rapidity of movement and alertness of mind are taught by various quickening exercises and games which require quick thinking and instantaneous muscular response. Boxing, wrestling, and all kinds of rough-and-tumble fighting play an important role in the development of the individual.

TEAMWORK.

4. While actual bayonet combat is individual, each man must understand from the very first that he is fighting for his side and not for himself alone. It follows, therefore, that he must be familiar with the tactical employment of the bayonet. He must not only know how, but when and when not to use it. For instance, it is absurd for a bayonet man to chase a retreating enemy and stab him in the back; he has a bullet in his rifle for just that purpose.

Again, the man who, forgetting that he is only a member of the team, rushes ahead of his comrades is always needlessly killed, thus helping the enemy and wasting his own life, as well as the time and efforts of the country he is trying to serve. Perfect teamwork is required in order to have a good line in the attack, but it is of more importance there than on dress parade.

The bayonet man is frequently called upon to act as protector to his constant comrade, the grenade-thrower, who is practically unarmed. This one fact requires that the bayonet man be familiar with the tactics of both weapons—bayonet and grenade—in mopping-up parties, trench raids, shell holes, and assaulting waves.

The supreme test of a soldier's training is to demand of him that he hold a position at the point of the bayonet. In such cases he must know just how to coordinate himself with the grenadiers and machine-gunners. He must know just what kind of a counter charge to make and exactly when to start it.

Finally, there is for the instructor to consider the close relation between controlled rifle fire and the bayonet, the last—and perhaps the most important—phase of bayonet training.

Section 2
Equipment

5. The rifle must always be in good condition—clean, oiled, and in perfect working order. Care must be taken that the object representing the enemy be incapable of injuring the bayonet or butt. Only light sticks are to be used for parrying practice with the rifle.

The chief causes of injury to the bayonet are: Delivering a sweeping point instead of a true or direct point, failure to withdraw the bayonet clear of the dummy before advancing and placing the dummies on hard, unprepared ground.

Discs.

6. For practicing direction there must always be an aiming mark on the dummy. Cardboard discs, 3 inches in diameter, can be improvised for this purpose. By continually changing the position of the disc the life of the dummy can be considerably prolonged. Five or six circles can be painted on the dummies to take the place of discs; the discs, however, will always be used in competitions. A number of circles, painted white, make the best marks.

Dummies.

7. Dummies, representing in size the trunk of a body, should be constructed of brushwood whenever available; failing this, use sacks filled with the material at hand that will offer most resistance to penetration and withdrawal without injuring the bayonet. Dummies must be so suspended that they offer the most resistance to the attacker and at the same time can be easily replaced.

Withdrawal Boards.

8. The withdrawal board is an instrument used to impress upon the mind of the student the amount of resistance to be expected in withdrawing the bayonet after a thrust. It can be constructed of a barrel stave or other board of similar dimensions, hinged at the top to a 4 x 4-inch upright, the lower end being left free. The instructor causes the student to place his bayonet between the upright and the board, and then presses upon the free end of the board, thus clamping the bayonet between the board and the upright. The amount of pressure exerted by the instructor varies with the resistance which it is desired to illustrate.

Other Apparatus.

9. Service Rifle and Bayonet.—Scabbard on bayonet, except when practicing on dummies or withdrawal boards.

Plastrons, masks, and gloves—one set for each man.

The Training Stick is a light stick, 5 feet to 5 feet 6 inches long and ¾ inch to 1 inch in diameter, padded at one end and provided at the other with a light rope or wire thrusting ring having a diameter of 3 inches. One for each man.

The Wooden Rifle.—Same outline as the service rifle, except that the part which corresponds to the bayonet is in prolongation of the barrel, no attempt being made to have the bayonet below the barrel, as this would weaken the junction. The balance is the same as the service rifle, and the weight nearly the same. A tennis ball, fastened to the end by canvas strips, makes the best pad. Hair or excelsior will answer. One for each man.

Unless this very important part of a soldier's training equipment becomes an article of issue, it can be sawed out of a piece of timber 2" x 6" x 5', and trimmed into shape by hand. The length of the wooden rifle, with tennis ball attached, can be made the same as the Model 1917 rifle, with bayonet fixed. No effort should be made to use the present fencing rifle. It is worse than useless.

Boxing gloves and a wrestling mat are essential parts of the equipment. They are indispensable in developing close and rough-and-tumble fighting.

PLATE 1-A.—DUMMIES AND COMBAT EQUIPMENT.

TRENCH SYSTEM.

10. There must be one or more trench systems for use in the assault training, trench and obstacle jumping, mopping-up parties, trench raiding, and, in general, for the tactical application of the principles of the bullet, bayonet and grenade combined.

No effort is, or should be, made to prescribe a type trench system. The instructor knows now what he wants; the details are left to his own ingenuity. If the terrain is suitable for the construction of dug-outs, moving and pendulum targets, dummies, etc., a combined course will easily result.

The proper construction and upkeep of the dummies and the repair of the assault training courses form part of the duties of the officers directly responsible for this part of the training.

SECTION 3

Special Features of the Bayonet and Suggestions to Instructors on Carrying Out Bayonet Training

REQUIREMENTS OF GOOD BAYONET WORK.

11. To attack effectively with the bayonet requires *nerve, good direction, strength,* and *quickness* during a state of wild excitement and probably physical exhaustion.

KILLING RANGE.

12. The maximum killing range of the bayonet is about 5 feet (measured from opponent's eyes to your own), but more often the killing is at closer quarters—at 2 feet or less—when troops are struggling *corps à corps* in the trenches or darkness.

BAYONET AN OFFENSIVE WEAPON.

13. Remember always that the bayonet is essentially an offensive weapon. Rush straight at an opponent with the point threatening his throat and deliver the thrust wherever an opening presents itself. If no opening is obvious, one must be made by deflecting the opponent's piece or by threatening him on one side and driving in on the other. But keep boring in. The man who fails to take advantage of an opening of one-fifth of a second in which to thrust may lose his life.

In a bayonet assault all ranks go forward *to kill or be killed,* and only those who have developed skill and strength by constant training will be able to kill.

There is no sentiment about the use of the bayonet. It is a cold-blooded proposition. The bayonet fighter *kills or is killed.* Few bayonet wounds come to the attention of the surgeon.

LENGTH OF LESSONS AND PRACTICE.

14. As it is not the intention nor is it necessary to make the technique of bayonet fighting difficult, long detail is quite unnecessary, and serves only to make the work (monotonous. All instruction must be carried out on common-sense lines. It should seldom be necessary to give a demonstration more than two or three times, after which the

TARGET PIT

SUPPORT TRENCH

150 YDS

COMMUNICATING
TRENCH

1ST LINE

150 YDS

TAKE OFF TRENCH

SECTION OF
BOYAUX

SECTION OF
TAKE OFF TRENCH
1ST LINE TRENCH
COMMUNICATING AND
SUPPORT TRENCH

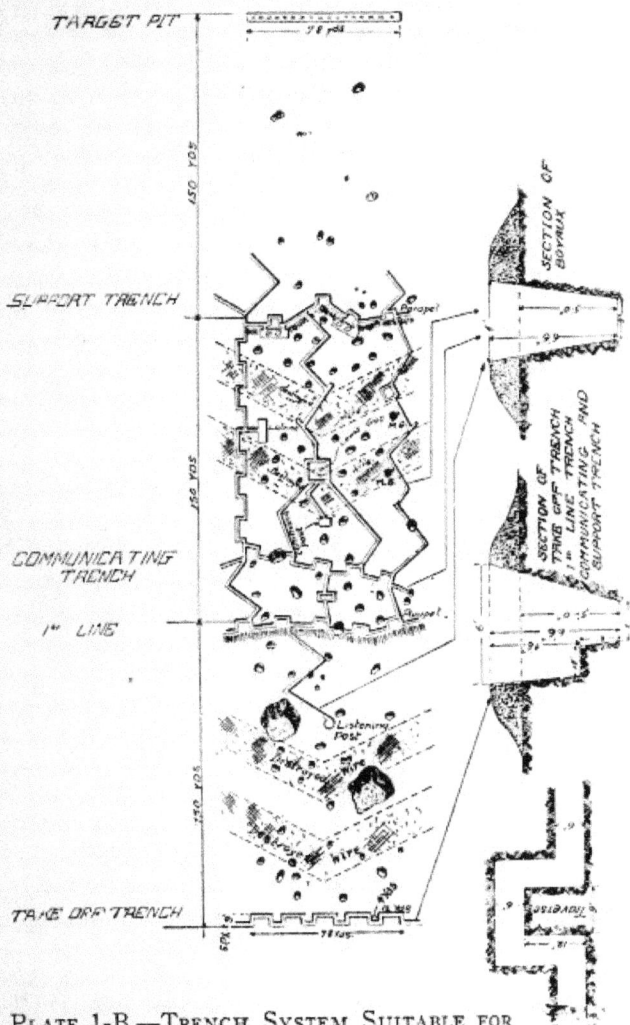

PLATE 1-B.—TRENCH SYSTEM SUITABLE FOR
ASSAULT TRAINING, AND COMBINED TAC-
TICS OF RIFLE, BAYONET AND GRENADE.

individual should acquire the correct position by practice. For this reason, a lesson or daily practice should rarely last more than one hour, given in two parts of half an hour each. Remember that nothing kills interest so quickly as monotony.

Strive for simplicity in all explanations. Do not quibble over minutiae. Insist on basic principles only. Each man has his own individual way of fighting.

Work Made Interesting.

15. Interest in the work is to be created by explaining the reasons for the various positions, the method of handling the rifle and bayonet, and the uses of the thrusts. Questions should be put to the men in order to ascertain whether or not they understand these reasons. When men realise the object of their work, they naturally take a greater interest in it. The instructor must have the men consider him a trainer and helper Competitions arouse and maintain interest in the work.

Progression.

16. Under the plan as herein prescribed, the work is carefully divided into successive steps, and this progression must not be delayed in order to obtain correct positions and good direction. These points having been properly covered in the instruction, their proficiency, quickness, and strength result from continual practice.

Physical Development.

17. Every officer and soldier must be brought to the highest state of physical development and kept in that condition. A man must train with the bayonet as a champion trains for a contest in which his title is at stake.

In order to encourage dash and gradually strengthen the leg muscles, from the beginning of the training all classes should be practiced in charging short distances, jumping trenches and hurdles, jumping in and vaulting out of trenches, etc.

Classes for Officers and Non-Commissioned Officers.

18. All company officers and non-commissioned officers must be trained as bayonet instructors in order that they may be able to teach their men this very important part of a soldier's training, which must be regularly practiced during the whole of the service at home and during the rest periods behind the firing line.

Conduct of Classes.

19. The class is always formed in two ranks facing each other, with a two-pace interval. The instructor goes wherever necessary, but while demonstrating a movement he should station himself to one flank and in prolongation of the centre line between ranks.

Each lesson is begun with a series of quickening movements, exercises, or games (all men like to play games) which develop coordination of the muscles used in bayonet combat. After combat practice, the instructor should review movements taught in the recruit course and correct all errors in detail. This will correct faults induced by simulated individual fighting.

20. Since the bayonet will be used in trenches which turn at the traverses, communication trenches, etc., to the right as well as to the left, it is necessary to teach men to use the rifle with either hand in front. This in order always to present the bayonet to the enemy before the body.

Men learn to use the piece left-handed (right hand in front) with but little practice, and many prefer it. It has the advantage of placing the stronger arm in front, where it directs the piece better and adds strength to the parries.

Size of Class.

21. The maximum number of men to be instructed by one trainer is twenty; better results will be obtained with classes of ten. Each man requires individual instruction and supervision. Large classes make this impossible.

To Teach a Position.

22. First demonstrate the position and explain all essential points, giving reasons for them. Then show the position again, making the class observe each movement, so that from the very beginning of his training a man is taught to use his eyes and brain. Order the class to assume and practice the position just explained. Pick out the man who shows the best position and have the class look at and copy him. His position will not be ideal, but it is more nearly correct than those assumed by the remainder, who, being beginners, cannot distinguish between a good position and an ideal one.

Do not make the mistake of trying to get a class of beginners to idealise at once; only by constant practice and continual correction can perfection be obtained.

For closer personal instruction, the instructor may call out the men by pairs, letting the others practice at will the positions and movements already taught.

Do everything you can to encourage the men to practice with the bayonet, training stick, etc., while off duty around barracks or camp, while at rest during other drills, etc. Utilise your own rest periods for short talks on the use and spirit of the bayonet.

SIGNALS.

23. In practicing the various movements, the use of signals should be begun as early as practicable. Their object is to coordinate the eyes with the muscles, thus training the men to see and to avail themselves quickly of openings. The signals were devised to supersede the vicious custom of turning bayonet work into a drill by the use of commands, which deadens a soldier's initiative and ignores the training of his eye.

These signals are not imitations of the movements they call for; imitations would be of little advantage to the pupil. The idea is to indicate with the trainer's hand an opening which the pupils perceive and act upon.

The signals, easily learned, will be used by the men working in pairs—one signalling, the other thrusting, etc.

To signal for the following positions or movements, the trainer moves as indicated:

Guard.—Assume it, left hand at back, right elbow at side, right forearm pointing to front, fist closed.

Short Guard.—Same as guard, except that the arm is drawn straight to the rear until the fist is at the right side.

Long Thrust.—Clap the right palm, fingers apart and extended, to that part of the body toward which the soldier is to aim.

Short Thrust.—Same as long thrust, except the fist is closed. If pupil is not in position of short guard when he gets the signal, he comes to that position and executes short thrust.

Jab.—Place both closed fists under the chin.

Parry.—Strike a blow diagonally across the body in the direction the parry is to be made, fist closed. Follow by signal for thrust.

Butt Strokes,—Make an upper cut with the fist to indicate a butt stroke to the crotch, a right hook for butt stroke to the jaw, an overhand swing for butt stroke to the head.

Slash (following butt stroke).—After butt stroke signal, carry the hand upward, fingers extended and joined, and slash down.

Disengage,—Describe an arc with the right hand, fingers extended and joined, in the direction the disengage is to be made. Make the arc with a forward motion. Follow by signal for thrust.

Cut-Over.—Describe an arc up and forward with the right hand, fingers extended and joined, in the direction the cut-over is to foe made. Follow by signal for thrust. In executing the movements, the point of the bayonet follows the movement of the trainer's hand, regardless of the relative right or left. When the trainer wishes the pupil to step forward with the rear foot in making any of the movements, the trainer steps to the rear as he gives the signal.

Section 4

General Instructions for Bayonet Training

Practice and Combat.

24. (*a*) Scabbards will not be removed from the bayonet except for thrusting at dummies and practice at withdrawal boards.

(*b*) The guard, withdrawal, thrusts, parries, and the jab will be taught first with the left, then the right, foot forward. Later the men must become ambidextrous in handling the rifle.

(*c*) The withdrawal position after a long thrust is the starting position for a short thrust. The short thrust naturally follows a long thrust.

(*d*) From the outset the class will be practiced frequently in making short charges in the open. This is a good quickening exercise, and it also develops the leg muscles.

(*e*) A target to thrust at will always be named when working by command; or if by signal, by position of hand or training stick; it will also be clearly marked on all dummies.

(*f*) Ranks working together must always be far enough apart to prevent accidents when thrusts are being made. When thrusts are made advancing, the ranks will change positions by coming to high port, double timing past each other and turning about. When working against dummies men will always continue the movement past the dummies, which they will leave on their right.

(*g*) The withdrawal, once taught, will be made after each thrust. After a thrust, advancing rear foot or on the advance, the hand will always be moved up the rifle on the withdrawal.

(*h*) The padding of the training stick will be as small as is consistent with safety.

(*i*) In the second practices the thrusts will also be practiced deliberately and progressively on dummies placed, as a preparation for assault training, in positions of increasing difficulty, *e.g.*, on parapets and steps of shallow trenches and in fire and communicating trenches.

(*j*) The entire five lessons will be taught right-handed before any left-handed practice is allowed.

(*k*) Jumping will usually be done from the high port by throwing the piece sharply to the front on taking off and bringing it back in on landing. Some men jump hurdles very easily by, holding the rifle in the guard position and throwing it up quickly on taking off. The grasp of the hands remains the same, and the piece is started down again when the man is at the highest point in his jump, thus bringing him down in a good position for thrusting. This applies the principle of jumping with weights. (Plate 2.)

PLATE 2.—JUMPING.

25. The system of training herein prescribed is based on the direct appeal to the student's brain through his eye, his natural instinct being utilised to the greatest extent, and the maximum amount of time being spent in practicing at will what has been shown him by the instructor. Instruction by demonstration rather than by word of command is to be the invariable method.

26. Each detail, after receiving individual instruction, will double-time back to its place in ranks, and will practice what they have been previously taught, correcting one another's faults.

At least once during each lesson the class should be formed in two ranks for the following exercise: As the instructor, who carries a training stick, approaches each man, that man will come to guard and threaten the instructor with his point as long as he is sufficiently near to attack. If the instructor holds the padded end above his waist line, a parry is required; if below, a butt stroke or kick. If the ring is presented, a thrust is required. The stick is "dead" when the ring is on the ground.

27. The following sequence will be adhered to in each lesson: All instruction will first be demonstrated to the class by the instructor with a man, at a dummy or with a training stick. The class, in class formation, will then practice at will all they have previously learned while the instructor gives each detail of two men individual instruction in the present lesson. The size of details may later be increased, according to the proficiency of the class. At the conclusion of the hour the instructor may review previous lessons by words of command.

28. The instructor must encourage the men to cultivate a facial expression of sternness, strength, eagerness to fight, and confidence in winning.

Section 5

Training Outlined and Movements Explained in Detail

29. Bayonet training may be divided into:

(*a*) The recruit course, which consists of five lessons, and assault training.

(*b*) The trained soldiers' daily practice, which constantly reviews the principles taught the recruit and combines the assault with musketry and grenade warfare.

30. The recruit course is so arranged that after six weeks service he will be able to begin the assault training. (Note: It is assumed that the first two weeks of a recruit's service will be given over to drawing equipment, vaccinations, inoculations, etc.) He will receive one hour instruction each day, given in two parts of half an hour each. The men will wear only such clothing as will permit freedom of movement in the training. Shoes should be hobbed in order to prevent slipping. Helmets, belts and packs may be required in tests and competitions.

Lesson 1: Vulnerable Parts of Body

31. The point of the bayonet should be directed against an opponent's throat, especially in hand-to-hand fighting, so that the point will enter easily and make a fatal wound on penetrating a few inches.

Also being near the opponent's face, it tends to make him flinch. Other vulnerable and usually exposed parts are the face, chest, lower abdomen, thighs, and, when the back is turned, the kidneys. The armpit, which may be reached with a jab, if the throat is protected, is vulnerable because it contains large blood vessels and a nerve centre.

Four to six inches penetration is enough to incapacitate and allow a quick withdrawal, whereas if a bayonet is driven home too far it is often impossible to withdraw it. In such cases a round must be fired to break up the obstruction.

GUARD.

32. Point of the bayonet directed at the base of the opponent's throat, the rifle, not canted, held firmly but not rigidly with both hands, the left hand, palm against side of rifle, at the most convenient position in front of the rear sight so that the left arm is only slightly bent, the right hand, palm to the left and just over the navel, grasping the small of the stock, the right forearm pressing the upper part of the butt to the body, legs separated as in taking a natural step and meeting with resistance, left foot leading, left knee slightly bent, feet separated laterally a few inches and both feet flat on the ground, toes pointed as the man naturally points them in walking. The weight is balanced over both legs.

The position must not be constrained in any way, but must be one of aggression, alertness, and readiness to go forward for instant attack. The guard position will also be taught with the right foot in front. (Plate 3.)

PLATE 3.—GUARD.

Reasons.

The point of the bayonet is directed at the base of the opponent's throat because that is the most vulnerable part of the body. The rifle is held with both hands to give the greatest strength. The barrel is up; *i.e.* "not canted," because this is the most offensive way of holding it. The palms of the hands are against the sides of the rifle because in this position the piece is not canted, and also the wrists are not bent in making the parries.

The hands are in the positions described because they give the best grip of the rifle and get it well advanced toward the opponent so that he can be reached with a minimum movement of the rifle; at the same time sufficient play is allowed to run him through. The legs are separated as in taking a natural step and meeting with resistance because this is what actually happens to a man in bayonet combat. Separating the feet laterally a few inches gives the man a broader and firmer base. The position is not constrained because if it were the muscles would soon tire and freedom of motion would be lost.

Common Faults.

(1) Leaning body back.

(2) Left arm too much bent, or too straight.

(3) Right hand held too low and too far back.

(4) Rifle grasped too rigidly, restraining all freedom of motion.

SHORT GUARD.

Left hand grasping rifle just under stocking swivel, left arm slightly bent, right hand grasping small of stock, stock against right hip. Point directed at base of opponent's throat. Body, legs, and feet as in guard.

REST.

33. Assume a position of rest in the easiest way without moving the feet. (Plate 4.)

HIGH PORT.

34. From the position of guard, without changing the grasp of the hands, carry the piece diagonally across the body until the left wrist is level with and in front of the left shoulder.

When jumping ditches, surmounting obstacles, etc., the position of the piece is approximately maintained with the left hand alone, leaving the right hand free. The high port is adopted only when actually preparing to assault. At other times the rifle is carried on the shoulder, at the trail, or slung, according to circumstances.

PLATE 4.—REST.

LONG THRUST.

35. Grip the rifle with all your strength and vigorously deliver the point from the guard position to the full extent of the left arm, extending quickly the whole body to the front, butt running along the inside of and against the right forearm. If in making the thrust the right elbow is carried low, so as to clamp the butt between the right forearm and the right side of the body, it furnishes a brace against the point being forced aside. In delivering the thrust the butt remains between the right forearm and the body.

The leading knee and ankle are well bent, the rear leg braced with the heel raised, the body inclined well forward.

The power of a thrust comes from the right arm, the shoulders, the back, the legs, and the weight of the body. The left arm is used more to direct the point of the bayonet. A delivered thrust throws a man off his balance, but in fighting this is instantly recovered by stepping forward with the rear foot. After a man has learned the details of a thrust it will always be delivered while advancing. *The eyes must be fixed on the object at which the thrust is made.*

In making thrusts other than straight to the front, the leading foot should move laterally in the same direction in which the thrust is made.

The long thrust is made at an opponent at a range of about 5 feet from the attacker's eye. It is very important to be able to judge this distance. In advancing on a dummy, men are prone to let the momentum of the body carry the point through the dummy without making the thrust. This must be guarded against, as it brings your point forward at the same rate of speed as your body, which is fairly uniform and easily judged. The darting forward of the point at the last instant gives a speed that is harder to judge. (Plate 5.)

PLATE 5.—LONG THRUST.

Reasons.

The rifle is gripped hard because the point, in entering the body, will meet with great resistance. The leading knee and ankle are well bent, the rear leg braced with the heel raised and the body inclined well forward, because in this position the maximum amount of reach and power are obtained in the thrust. The rear foot is always brought forward in order to preserve the balance, and also because the thrust will usually be made advancing. The eyes must be fixed on the object aimed at in order to secure a hit.

Common Faults.

(1) Rifle drawn back just before delivering thrust.
(2) Elbow and butt of rifle held as high as or against the right shoulder.
(3) Eyes not directed at object.
(4) Leading knee not sufficiently bent.
(5) Body not inclined forward enough.
(6) Failure of point to go forward on a straight line.
(7) Butt not braced against inside of right forearm.
(8) Doing too much work with the arms and not getting the body into it.

36. To withdraw the bayonet after a "long thrust" has been delivered, jerk the rifle straight back until the right hand is behind the hip, this without unduly relaxing the grasp of the small of the stock, and immediately resume the "guard" position.

Don't try to do all the work with your arms. Carry the weight of your body to the rear by straightening out the leading leg and straightening the body up at the waist. Yank the piece to the rear with the shoulders and arms.

If the leverage or proximity to the object transfixed renders it necessary, the left hand must first be slipped toward the muzzle, and when a pupil reaches the stage of delivering a "thrust" while advancing on a dummy or thrusting ring, he will adopt this method.

After every thrust, make a rapid withdrawal before coming to guard. A quick withdrawal is necessary to get ready to meet another enemy, to prevent the one just stuck from bending your bayonet in falling, and to prevent him attempting to injure you. Men still have fight left in them after you stick them unless you hit a vital spot, but when the bayonet comes out and the air sucks in and they begin to bleed on the inside they feel the pain and lose their fight. (Plates 6A and 6-B.)

Common Faults.

(1) Not making withdrawal vigorously enough.

(2) Not drawing bayonet back on line of penetration, *i.e.*, letting butt drop.

FIRST PRACTICE, THRUSTING AT CHANGING TARGETS.

37. The class, working in pairs, with the instructor supervising, should be practiced in thrusting in various directions, *e. g.* (1) at the opposite man's hand, which is placed in various positions on and off the body; (2) at thrusting, rings, etc., tied on the ends of sticks. This practice must be done without word of command.

SECOND PRACTICE, THRUSTING AT DISCS ON DUMMIES.

38. The men will be taught to transfix a disc or circle painted on a dummy, first from a halt at a distance of about 5 feet from the dummy (*i.e.*, the extreme range of the bayonet), and then, after advancing three or more paces, later increasing the distance and speed as the men progress.

The advance must be made in a practical and natural way, and

PLATE 6-A.—WITHDRAWAL FROM
LONG THRUST.

PLATE 6-B.—WITHDRAWAL FROM
LONG THRUST AT PRONE DUMMY.

should be practiced with either foot to the front when the thrust is
delivered. The rifle must never be drawn back just before making a
thrust in a forward movement. The impetus of the body and the forward stretching of the arms supply the maximum force.

The bayonet must be withdrawn immediately after the thrust has
been delivered and a forward threatening attitude assumed to the side
of or beyond the dummy.

Unless the rifle is firmly gripped, it is liable to injure the hand. By
gripping the rifle as far back on the small of the stock as the comb
will permit, the forefinger will be saved from being cut by the trigger
guard.

To guard against accidents, the men must be at least 5 feet apart
when the practice is carried out collectively.

117

The principles of this practice will be observed while thrusting at dummies in trenches, standing upright on the ground, or suspended from gallows. They should be applied at first slowly and deliberately, for no attempt must be made to carry out the assault training before the men have been carefully instructed in and have thoroughly mastered the preliminary lessons.

LEFT
LOW.

RIGHT.

RIGHT
LOW.

LEFT.

FROM
PARAPET.

FROM
TRENCH.

PLATES 7-A, B, AND C.—PARRIES.

LESSON 2: THE PARRIES

PARRY RIGHT (LEFT).

39. From the position of guard, vigorously straighten the left arm without bending the wrists or twisting the rifle in the hands, at the same time engaging opponent's piece and deflecting it just clear of your body, forcing your body forward to the full extent of your reach. Keep the barrel up, the point threatening the opponent's body, preferably his throat. If the parry right is properly made, it is easy to kill the opponent with the thrust which immediately follows—in fact, the opponent will usually impale himself on your point.

In parry left the point is carried out of line with your opponent's body, but can be quickly brought back, as it is nearer this line than the opponent's point. Parry left is followed up at once either with a thrust or a butt stroke to the ribs or jaw. During the parry the eyes must be kept on the point of the weapon being parried, but, having completed the parry, the eyes are instantly fixed on the part of the opponent's body to be attacked. (Plates 7-A, 7-B, and 7-C.)

FENDING OFF.

In addition, practice must be given in fending off the opponent's point with *either bayonet or rifle in any position.*

Common Faults.

(1) Wide sweeping parry with no forward movement in it.
(2) Eyes taken off the point of the weapon to be parried.
(3) Making the arms do all the work and not getting the weight, strength, and momentum of the body into the parry.
(4) Parry lacking force.

Men should be taught to regard the parry as an offensive movement.

Parries will be practiced with the right as well as with the left foot forward preparatory to the practice of parrying when advancing.

Men when learning the parries should be made to observe the movements of the rifle carefully, and should not be kept longer at this practice than is necessary for them to understand what is required; that is, vigorous, yet controlled, action.

FIRST PRACTICE.

The class works in pairs, with scabbards on bayonets: one man thrusts with a stick and the other parries. The "guard" position is resumed after each parry.

At first this practice must be slow and deliberate without letting it become mechanical. It will be increased in rapidity and vigour as the instruction progresses.

Care must be taken that the man thrusting with the stick does not swing it into the man with the rifle. If the man makes sweeping movements with the stick, the man with the rifle will probably develop sweeping parries.

PLATE 8-A.—SHORT THRUST.

PLATE 8-B.—WITHDRAWAL FROM SHORT THRUST.

SECOND PRACTICE.

Sticks long enough to represent the opponent's weapon in the "guard" position should be attached to the dummies and parried.

The men must also be taught to parry thrusts made at them (1) by an "enemy" in a trench when they are themselves on the parapet; (2) by an "enemy" on the parapet when they are in the trench, and (3) when both are fighting on the same level at close quarters in a deep trench.

LESSON 3: THE SHORT THRUST

40. Shift the left hand quickly towards the muzzle and draw the rifle back to the extent of the right arm, this without unduly relaxing the grasp of the small of the stock, the butt either upwards or downwards, according as a low or a high thrust is to be made; then deliver the thrust vigorously to the full extent of the left arm.

N. B.—The short thrust is used at a range of about 3 feet, and in close fighting it is the natural thrust made when the bayonet has just been withdrawn after a long thrust. If a strong withdrawal is necessary, the right hand should be slipped above the rear sight after the "short thrust" has been made. (Plates 8A and 8-B.)

PRACTICE.

41. The principles of the two practices of Lesson I should be observed so far as they apply. By placing a disc on each of the dummies, the "short thrust" may be taught in conjunction with the "long thrust," the first disc being transfixed with the long, the second with the short thrust. On delivery of the "long thrust," if the left foot is forward, the "short thrust" would take place with the right foot forward, and *vice versa*.

"Fend off" will be practiced from the position of the "short thrust."

LESSON 4: THE JAB

42. From the position of the short thrust, shift the right hand up the rifle and grasp it above the rear sight, at the same time bringing the rifle to an almost vertical position close to the body, and from this position bend the knees, and, with the full force of the body, stepping in if necessary, jab the point of the bayonet upwards into the throat or other part of the opponent. (Plate 9.)

Reasons.

The rifle is carried almost to a vertical position, jab is used only in close fighting and when embraced by an opponent, and will be made usually at the upper part of opponent's body (throat or armpit). The knees are bent in order to allow the body to impart a powerful upward movement to the bayonet.

Common Faults.

(1) Rifle drawn backward and not held upright enough.

(2) Rifle grasped too low with the right hand.

(3) Doing all the work with the arms and not putting the whole body into it.

(4) Not pressing the rifle against the leg.

(5) Jab not vigorous enough and too high.

From the "jab" position men will be practiced in fending off an attack made at any part of them.

The "jab" is employed in close-quarter fighting in narrow trenches and when "embraced" by an opponent.

After any move that carries the point beyond the enemy, if possible, come immediately to the short thrust or jab position; that is, keep your point between you and your enemy.

PLATE 9.—JAB.

LESSON 5: METHODS OF INJURING AN OPPONENT

43. It should be impressed upon the class that, although a man's "thrust" has missed or has been parried, or his bayonet has been broken, he can, as "attacker," still maintain his advantage by injuring his opponent.

In individual fighting the butt can also be used horizontally against the opponent's jaw, etc. This method is impossible in trench fighting or in an attack, owing to the horizontal sweep of the bayonet to the attacker's left. In many instances a kick to kneecap or crotch will aid the butt stroke.

A butt stroke or kick will only temporarily disable an enemy, who must be immediately killed with the bayonet.

It should be clearly understood that the butt must not be employed when it is possible to use the point of the bayonet effectively.

TRENCH OR VERTICAL BUTT STROKES.

44. *Butt Stroke 1.*—Swing up the butt at the opponent's crotch, ribs, forearm, etc., using a half-arm blow, advancing with the rear foot.

Butt Stroke 2.—If the opponent jumps back so that the first butt stroke misses, the rifle will come into a horizontal position over the left shoulder, butt leading. The attacker will then step in with the rear foot and dash the butt into his opponent's face.

Butt Stroke 3.—If the opponent retires still further out of distance, the attacker again closes up and slashes his bayonet down on the opponent's head or neck, the latter if he is wearing a steel helmet. In the event of missing, he will then be in the guard position.

Butt Stroke 4.—If the point is beaten or brought down, the butt can be used effectively by crashing it down on the opponent's head with an over-arm blow, advancing the rear foot. When the opponent is out of distance Butt Stroke 3 can again be used. (Plates 10-A and 10-B.)

OPEN GROUND OR HORIZONTAL BUTT STROKES

45. *Butt Stroke 1.*—Advancing the rear foot, with a half-arm blow swing the butt up at opponent's jaw.

Butt Stroke 2.—If the opponent jumps back so that the first stroke misses the rifle will come into a horizontal position over the left shoulder, butt leading. The attacker will then step in with the rear foot and slash the bayonet into opponent's face.

If the opponent retires further out of distance, the attacker will now be in the guard position.

46. Butt Stroke 1 is essentially a half-arm blow from the shoulder, keeping the elbow rigid, and it can, therefore, be successfully employed only when the right hand is grasping the rifle at the small of the stock.

47. Butt strokes can only be used in certain circumstances and positions, but if men acquire absolute control of their weapons under these conditions, they will be able to adapt themselves to all other phases of in-fighting. For instance, when a man is gripped by an op-

123

PLATE 10-A.—Vertical Butt Stroke No. 1.

PLATE 10-B.—Horizontal Butt Stroke No. 1

ponent so that neither the point nor the butt can be used, the knee, brought up against the crotch or the heel stamped on the instep, may momentarily disable him and make him release his hold.

48. When the classes have been shown the methods of using the kick, the rifle butt, and the knee, they should be practiced on the stick, *e.g.*, fix several discs on a dummy and make a thrust art one, use the knee on another fixed low down, jab a third, and so on.

Light dummies should be used for practice with the butt, in order to avoid damage to it.

49. For other methods of injuring an opponent, see *Hand-to-Hand Fighting*, published by the Infantry School of Arms for use in training the United States Army.

To Disarm an Opponent.

50. Fend off opponent's thrust with your right hand. Step forward and seize his left hand with both of yours, your left under his palm, your right over his fingers. Give a sharp twist outward.

51. Parry opponent's thrust with your left hand. Step in and seize his left wrist firmly with your right hand; grasp the rifle just below the bayonet with your left hand, back of hand down, and swing it violently upward and over to the right, at the same time stepping in and kicking or bringing your left knee into the lower part of your opponent's body.

52. Parry opponent's thrust outward with your right hand; stepping in, kick him in the crotch or on the shin. Grasp the rifle just below the bayonet with your right hand, back of hand down, and swing it upward and over to the left; force the point of the bayonet to the ground, and, stepping in, back-heel your opponent.

Summary of Lessons.

53. *Lesson 1*:

(1) Short talk on use and spirit of the bayonet.

(2) Explain vulnerable parts of body.

(3) Take class to withdrawal boards and show them the necessity for a strong jerk in withdrawing. Then let class practice same sharp jerk on withdrawal from dummy.

(4) Fall class in. Explain and cause them to take the usual formation for instruction. Demonstrate guard. Class practices this while instructor corrects faults.

(5) Demonstrate high port from guard. Advancing in guard position short charge, quickening exercise.

(6) Demonstrate long thrust, getting full reach, withdrawal and return to guard. Class practice at will, slowly at first, then increasing speed, instructor correcting faults. Repeat at dummies, advancing long thrust at dummies, slipping left hand up to withdraw.

From now on all long thrusts will be made while advancing, the left hand being slipped up for the withdrawal.

(7) Thrusting at ring while advancing, hand slipped up for withdrawal as at dummies and either foot being brought up if necessary, to obtain movement of the hand. First demonstrated by instructor; then

done by the men, working in pairs, as master and pupil, and correcting each other's faults.

(8) Thrusting at hand, by signal. Same as (7).

Lesson 2.—Parries.

(9) Review Lesson 1.

(10) Demonstrate parries. Have class execute; instructor correct errors. High and low parries, taught from trench and parapet.

(11) Master and pupil, parries by signal.

(12) Man with rifle parry thrust from training stick. Thrust made very slowly at first.

(13) With training stick, parry thrust made by charging opponent.

Note.—Attacker starts at high port, then comes to guard, and when within about 5 feet of defender removes right or left hand, according to whether attack is made on left or right side. (Plate 11.)

(14) At dummies—advance, parry stick, and thrust (training stick attached to dummy to represent enemy's weapon).

PLATE 11.—ATTACKING WITH TRAINING STICK.

Lesson 3.—Short Thrust.

(15) Review previous lessons.

(16) Explain when used. Demonstrate at two dummies placed in suitable positions. (This should be done by instructor advancing, making long thrust, slipping left hand up and withdrawing. He is then in short-thrust position, and will deliver short thrust, advancing rear foot.)

(17) Advancing long thrust; withdraw, slipping up left hand; advancing, short thrust; withdraw, slipping up right hand under left. At hand by signal; at thrusting ring and at dummies.

(18) Fend off from short-thrust position.

126

Lesson 4.—Jab.

(19) Review previous lessons.

(20) Explain when used. Demonstrate at dummies. (Instructor advances, makes long thrust, withdraws; makes short thrust, withdraws; lowers butt and from this position delivers jab, advancing rear foot, if necessary.)

(21) Advancing long thrust, short thrust, and jab by hand signal, at thrusting ring and at dummies.

(22) Fend off from jab position.

Lesson 5.—Butt Strokes, etc.

(23) Review previous lessons.

(24) Explain and demonstrate vertical and horizontal butt strokes, using dummies.

(25) Butt strokes practiced by hand signal, at padded end of training stick and at dummies.

(26) Toe to knee, heel to instep and knee to crotch, using padded end of stick.

(27) Demonstrate disarming tricks, bone-breaking holds, etc.

54. Having completed the five lessons as above described, the recruit is ready to begin the assault training, reviewing each day, however, the movements of the recruit course.

Exercises Used in Obtaining Good Direction and Quickness

CIRCLE EXERCISES, HAND PARRIES, ETC.

55. (*a*) At the command "Form circle," the pupils, not more than ten in number, form in a circle, *facing* the trainer with an interval of about three paces, at the position of "guard," bayonet scabbards on. The trainer thrusts in varying order with the training stick at the pupils, who "parry" from the position of "guard," "short guard," and "jab," and thrust or rush in and jab at trainer, who retires rapidly.

(*b*) *Face the pupils about.*—At a touch from the "training stick," the pupil whirls about and attacks the thrusting ring with the thrust or jab, as the distance between his point and the stick indicates. If the ring is holed, the withdrawal is made and the position of "guard" resumed. If the first effort is a miss, the pupil will come on with "short thrust" and "jab" until successful.

If the trainer presents the padded end of the stick, the pupil makes butt stroke one at it. If this is a miss, he comes on with butt stroke two, etc., until he hits the padded end. As soon as he hits it he resumes the guard, facing out. To practice the pupil in all the butt strokes, the instructor jerks the stick away a short distance just before butt stroke one; hits it, causing the pupil to miss and come on with butt stroke two. Just before butt stroke two hits the stick, the trainer again jerks it away, causing the pupil to miss and come on with a slash. (Plate 12.)

PLATE 12.—CIRCLE EXERCISE.

(c) Men in pairs, one with rifle in guard position, the other on either side offers the ring or padded end of the stick in varying positions in front and behind. The man with the rifle attacks the stick as laid down in paragraph (b).

(d) To practice "long thrust," "short thrust," and "jab" against an opponent:

One line of men, with bayonets and scabbards placed at long thrusting distance before a line of men without arms.

The armed men make a long thrust, stepping in; at a hand signal made by the unarmed men, the latter step back and with the other hand fend the thrust, grab and hold the bayonet to give the withdrawal the necessary resistance.

At a second signal the attack is continued by the short thrust, stepping in, the retreat and fend repeated. The two men, now being at close quarters, a signal for "jab" is made, the defender grabbing the bayonet and resisting the stroke.

The fend should not be made with the hand indicating the point of attack. The signalling hand should remain in place as a point at which to aim. The signal should be made with the hand on the side of the body at which the attack is to be made. In this way the bayonet is quickly pushed outside the line of the body with the other hand.

WOODEN RIFLES AND PERSONAL COMBAT.

56. The wooden rifle, like boxing and wrestling, introduces into the training the most important element of personal contact, without which the true fighting spirit cannot be properly developed. The work with the wooden rifles is very slow and easy at first, the men gradually working up speed until they come together at full tilt. Gloves, masks, and plastrons will always be worn, and the instructor is responsible for the prevention of serious accidents.

Men begin this combat practice by both standing still; then one advances at a walk, the other standing still; then both advancing at a walk; then one man running, the other standing still, and, finally, both men advancing at a run.

DISENGAGE.

Drop the point of the bayonet slightly with the left hand and bring it up on the opposite side of the opponent's piece, coming in at the same time. The point should go forward about a foot in the act of passing under the enemy's rifle. (Plates 13-A, B, and C.) (*Note.*—If the opponent's point is held low, bring your piece to the opposite side by passing it over his. This is the "Cut Over.")

COMBAT PRACTICE—RUSHING.

57. Place two men 20 yards apart in the "guard" position. At signal, they charge each other. Unless a clean, hard hit is made in 20 seconds, they will be separated and a hit counted against each. Never allow men to fight for more than one hit in any assault.

Occasionally require men to hold the piece at "short-guard." This compels in-fighting

If, during the above rushing, there appear any of the following mistakes, fall out the responsible men and let the trainer work with them individually until they recover their form. All tendencies to wildness must be rigorously checked:

(*a*) Flagrant loss of aim or balance.

(*b*) Light tapping touches.

(*c*) Hitting with the side of the bayonet.

(*d*) Pushing with the rifle.

(*e*) Useless parries or movements of the rifle.

(*f*) Slowing up just before the shock.

PLATES 13-A, B, AND C.—DISENGAGE.

RUSHING IN GROUPS.

58. (1) Let one man receive the assault of two or three others, placed one behind the other at 10 or 15 paces distance.

(2) Let one man receive the assault of two others at 6 paces interval, converging upon his flank, at 20 paces.

(3) Let one man receive the assault of two others at 6 paces interval, converging upon him as they come in.

(4) Have men fight when one is in the trench and one on the para-

pet, and when both men are in a narrow trench.

(5) Vary these formations in any way that may appear valuable and instructive.

TEAM FIGHTING.

59. After the men have attained proficiency in individual combat, squad will be opposed to squad and platoon against platoon, as in the chapter on Assault Practice, men being substituted for dummies.

TRENCH COMBAT.

60. In trench combat, when you come to a turn in the trench, make a quick vault in the next sector of the trench. As you land in the next sector, have your rifle in the guard position (on the right side if the trench turned to the left, on the left side if it turned to the right), ready to beat your opponent's weapon aside or make a quick thrust.

There is nothing to be gained by looking first, and it ensures your enemy being ready for you. If you come to a place alone where one trench enters another about at right angles, it is well to look first, as one man has no show if there is an enemy on each side of the entrance.

If you find one side clear, vault in the other without delaying to look. If two men approach such a trench, say, through a communication trench, they approach as nearly on a line as the width of the trench will permit.

One vaults to the right and the other to the left without stopping to find out first whether the trench is occupied.

ASSAULT PRACTICE.

61. This must approximate as nearly as possible the conditions of actual fighting, and is not to be undertaken until the men have received thorough preliminary training and have acquired complete control of their weapons.

In any assault the attackers are necessarily subjected to severe physical exertion, as well as to a great nervous tension, while the defenders are comparatively fresh. Therefore, quick aim and good direction with the bayonet when attacking, while moving rapidly or surmounting obstacles, accurate and vigorous delivery of the thrust, and clean, quick withdrawals are of the greatest importance, and need the same careful attention and constant practice as are devoted to obtaining efficiency with the rifle.

In the assault practice the charge brings the man to the first trench in a comparatively exhausted condition, and the accuracy of the aim is tested by the disc, which can only be "carried" by a true and vigorous thrust and a clean withdrawal.

For this practice the men should be made to begin the assault from a trench 6 or 7 feet deep, as well as from the open, and they should not cheer until close up to the "enemy."

TRENCH SYSTEM FOR ASSAULT PRACTICE.

62. A reproduction of a labyrinth of trenches, with dummies in the "dugouts" and shelters between the trenches, forms an excellent assault practice course. Assaults should be made from all four sides in order to give variety.

The edges of the trenches should be protected by spars of baulks anchored back: otherwise constant use will soon wear them out. Cinders scattered over the course will prevent the men from slipping. If gallows cannot be erected, sack dummies should be placed on tripods or on end, as well as lying in trenches or on the parapet, with soft earth, free from stones, under them.

COMBINED TACTICS.

63. If a combined bullet and bayonet course is to be had, an ingenious instructor can arrange some very interesting and practical exercises by combining the tactics of the assault with those of other branches of infantry training.

TRAINING SOLDIERS DAILY PRACTICE.

64. One-half hour a day, on at least five days a week, should be devoted to the practice of bayonet fighting by trained soldiers. By this daily practice accuracy of direction, quickness, and strength are developed, and a soldier is accustomed to using the bayonet under conditions which approximate actual fighting. This half-hour will be given over largely to assault training, the instructor, however, going back to a short review of any part of the recruit course whenever he deems it necessary. This practice includes:

(*a*) Bayonet practice.

(*b*) Individual combat.

(*c*) Firing at moving, bobbing, and disappearing targets, and rapid fire.

(*d*) Counter-charging.

(*e*) Combination of musketry, bayonet, and grenade.

Section 6

Tactics of the Bayonet Combined Training

65. It has already been said that the bayonet is one of the most important weapons of the infantry. Therefore, in order to arrive at the correct use of the bayonet, we must bear constantly in mind just what tasks the infantry is called upon to perform. The artillery, with its heavy, long-range guns, is largely responsible for the process of "digging in," but it certainly cannot be expected to shoot the enemy out of position, once he is strongly entrenched. Only the infantry can gain ground, and, similarly, no position is lost until its defending infantry retires.

The sound, well-established tactical principles of the employment of infantry are today unchanged, but the present European War, (1918), has changed somewhat the application of those principles. Two long opposing lines, with flanks absolutely secure, make any large enveloping movement; impossible, and any attack, great or small, local or covering great areas, must be purely frontal.

The underlying idea of all infantry tactics is to close with the enemy as soon as possible and with all the units well in hand. The ideal conditions would be those making possible a quiet, quick, and orderly advance without halting to open fire, but this is impossible with the highly developed weapons of today, and even though some of the attacking infantry managed to close with the enemy, there would be too few left for a bayonet fight. Therefore, in order to make a successful assault, the infantry must move up under covering fire.

To provide this protecting fire, it has equipped itself with the pistol, bayonet, and high-powered rifle, the 1-pounder, trench mortars, the effective hand and rifle grenades, and has called to its assistance its supporting arm—the artillery. The enemy, attempting to protect himself from the terrific fire that he knows will precede the infantry attack, has prepared deep dugouts and bombproofs, in which he often hides until the last possible minute.

Despite the fact that all of the above preparations are simply to give the bayonet man a chance to use his weapon (and to kill as many of the enemy as possible while doing it), it follows that fire action is more important than shock action, for without the fire the shock would be impossible. Therefore, the bayonet men must know how to shoot their rifles and to cooperate with the machine gun, the grenade, and the artillery, and must be so formed that during the assault they can deliver an effective rifle fire, present a solid front to the enemy in the bayonet charge, and be close enough together to furnish mutual moral and physical support.

The wave attack that has been used so much in France was produced in order to furnish the greatest amount of mutual support among automatic riflemen, grenadiers, the 1-pounders, and riflemen, and at the same time to allow the greatest number of riflemen (bayonet men) to close with the enemy in the best formation possible. All of the conditions so far discussed make it imperative that the assaulting troops be perfectly organised, and that they follow their covering fire (barrage) as closely as possible.

As indicated above, the defenders are forced to retire to their dugouts, where they may easily remain too long. An attack has the best chance of succeeding when it can meet the defenders emerging from their dugouts, but if the assaulting troops are met by the defenders on their own parapet, the assault will probably fail. Thus a few seconds will turn the scales, and for that reason the assault must keep moving forward. If firing is possible, it must be done from the shoulder or hip while advancing.

The men must rise from the starting trench as one man and advance as one man. Thereafter the advance continues at a steady walk, except for the last 30 or 40 yards before reaching each trench, when the line breaks into a slow double time, finishing up the last few yards at a run and without yelling. This favours the surprise element. Once in the enemy's trench, shock action is impossible, and it is merely a question of our ability and will to use the bayonet.

The bayonet man, when working in the trenches with grenadiers, must cover their advance, prevent them from being rushed, and clear the way for further progress, never forgetting, in his desire to use the bayonet, that he is also master of the bullet. In the actual melee, however, the enemy must be killed with the bayonet, since the bullet would probably be as dangerous for friend as for foe.

Darkness or surprise effect sometimes replaces the covering fire. Surprise is always of great assistance to the bayonet man, and at night all available cover can be easily used, but long, careful training and frequent rehearsals of the particular attack are necessary to prevent confusion during night operations.

To sum up, the bayonet is only an offensive weapon, and its users must move over short distances straight up to the enemy's position and without halting to fire. All the other details of an assault are to give the bayonet man an opportunity to close with the enemy, and the success of an attack depends upon, first, whether or not sufficient men can reach the enemy, and, second, having closed with him, whether or not they are imbued with the spirit of the bayonet.

Any number of excellent combined problems may be worked out. The following are some that will prove particularly interesting and instructive. In the solution of these problems a trench system must be had, umpires used, and often it will be necessary to arrange distinguishing marks for opposing sides:

(1) A detachment of Reds is ordered to attack a certain point in a quiet Blue front line trench and capture one or more prisoners.

(2) The conduct of a Red detachment while driving a Blue detachment down Blue's communication trench to his second line trench.

(3) A Red patrol of bombers and bayonet men in No Man's Land at night unexpectedly encounters a Blue patrol.

(4) Reds have assaulted and taken a Blue position, and are engaged in consolidating it when Blues counter attack:

(*a*) Reds have plenty of ammunition.

(*b*) Reds have no ammunition.

(*Note.*—Reds may or may not have automatic rifle.)

(5) Defending Reds to meet assaulting Blues with a counter charge.

Bayonet Training

By William H. Waldron

The system of Bayonet Training stated herein is taken from the provisional Manual of Bayonet Training of the British Army. In the vernacular of the day, it is the "real dope."

Every battalion should have a bayonet assault practice course constructed along the lines indicated and the work of training should be systematically conducted. The non-commissioned officers should be taken out on a "Tactical Walk" on the course and all the features of the exercises explained. This is followed by their practical training over the course and this in turn is followed by the instruction of the privates of the organisation.

FEATURES OF THE BAYONET

To attack with the bayonet effectively requires good direction, strength and quickness, during a state of wild excitement and probable physical exhaustion. The limit of the range of a bayonet is about 5 feet (measured from the opponent's eyes) but more often the killing is at close quarters, at a range of 2 feet or less, when troops are struggling hand to hand in trenches or darkness.

The bayonet is essentially an offensive weapon—go straight at an opponent with the point threatening his throat and deliver the point wherever an opening presents itself. If no opening is obvious, one must be created by beating off the opponent's weapon or making a "feint point" in order to make him uncover himself.

Hand to hand fighting with the bayonet is individual, which means that a man must think and act for himself and rely on his own resources and skill; but, as in all games, he must play for his side and not only for himself.

In a bayonet assault all ranks go forward to kill or be killed, and only those who have developed skill and strength by constant training will be able to kill.

The spirit of the bayonet must be inculcated into all ranks so that they go forward with that aggressive determination and confidence of superiority born of continual practice, without which a bayonet assault will not be effective.

The technical points of bayonet fighting are extremely few and simple. The essence of bayonet training is continuity of practice.

Method of Carrying out Bayonet Training and Hints to Instructors

An important point to be kept in mind in Bayonet Training is the development of the individual by teaching him to think and act for himself.

The simplest means of attaining this end is to make men use their brains and eyes to the fullest extent by carrying out the practices so far as possible, without words of command, *i.e.*, to point at a shifting target as soon as it is stationary, to parry sticks, etc. The class should, whenever possible, work in pairs and act on the principle of "master and teacher."

This procedure in itself, develops individuality and confidence. Sharp jerky words of command which tend to make men act mechanically, should be omitted.

Rapidity of movement and alertness are taught by competition in fixing and unfixing the bayonet and by other such quickening movements.

As the technique of bayonet fighting is so simple, long detail is quite unnecessary and makes the work monotonous. All instructions should be carried out on common-sense lines. It should seldom be necessary to give the details of a "point" or "parry" more than two or three times, after which the class should acquire the correct positions by practice. For this reason, a lesson or daily practice should rarely last more than half an hour. Remember that nothing kills interest so easily as monotony.

The spirit of the bayonet is to be inculcated by describing the special features of bayonet and hand to hand fighting. The men must learn to practice bayonet fighting in the spirit and with the enthusiasm that animates them when training for their games, and to look upon their instructor as a trainer and helper. Interest in the work is to be created by explaining the reasons for the various positions, the method of handling the rifle and bayonet and the uses of the points.

Questions should be put to the men to find out if they understand these reasons. When men realise the object of their work, they naturally take a greater interest in it.

Progression in bayonet training is regulated by obtaining first correct position and good direction, then quickness. Strength is the outcome of continual practice.

In order to encourage dash and gradually strengthen the leg muscles from the commencement of the training, classes should be frequently practiced in charging short distances over the bayonet practice courses.

All company officers and non-commissioned officers should be taught how to instruct in bayonet training in order that they may be able to teach their squads and platoons this very important part of a soldier's training, which must be regularly practiced during the whole of his service at home, and during his periods of rest behind the firing-lines.

The greatest care should be taken that the object representing the opponent and its support should be incapable of injuring the bayonet or butt. Only light sticks are to be used for parrying practice.

The chief causes of injury to the bayonet are insufficient instruction, in the bayonet training lessons, failure to withdraw the bayonet clear of the dummy, and placing the dummies on hard, unprepared ground.

Formation.—Intervals or distances are taken as prescribed in paragraphs 109 and 111 I. D. R. Bayonets are fixed, paragraph 95, I. D. R.

Technique of Instruction.—Before requiring the soldier to take a position or execute a movement for the first time, the instructor should show him the position or how to execute the movement, stating the essential elements and explaining the purpose that they serve.

Illustrate the position or movement a second time, requiring careful observation so that the men will be taught to use their eyes and brains right from the beginning.

Now, require the men to assume the position or execute the movement under consideration. Accuracy and expertness will be developed by practice.

Fatigue and exhaustion should be carefully guarded against. They prevent proper interest being taken in the exercises and delay the progress of the instruction.

The training consists of five lessons and the Final Assault practice.

Lesson No. 1

The First lesson is divided into:

1. The position of *Guard*, from which the various bayonet attacks are made.

2. The position of *High Port*, which is assumed when advancing.

3. The *Long Point*, which is the normal method of bayonet attack.

4. The *Withdrawal*, which follows the attack.

The Position of Guard

Being at the Order Arms: Raise the piece with the right hand, throw it to the front. Grasp with both hands, the left at a convenient place above the rear sight so that the left arm is only slightly bent; right hand at the small of the stock and held just in front of the navel. The rifle is held naturally and easily, without constraint, barrel inclined slightly to the left.

At the same time the left foot is carried forward to a point in a natural position such as a man walking might adopt on meeting with resistance. The left knee is slightly bent, right leg straight and braced. The right foot is flat on the ground with the toe inclined to the right front.

The common faults that will be noted in assuming the position are:

1. The body will be leaned back from the hips, which causes unsteadiness and does not permit quick and aggressive action.

2. The left arm is bent too much, which raises the point of the bayonet too high and produces a certain amount of constraint. The left hand should grasp the piece at such a point that will avoid this defect. A little practice will show the exact place to hold the hand to obtain the maximum effect.

3. The right hand may be held too low and too far back, which has the effect of raising the point of the bayonet and giving a faulty position to the left arm and hand.

4. The rifle may be grasped too tightly with the hands, which produces rigidity and restrains freedom of movement. The left hand merely guides the bayonet in the attack, the right furnishes the power behind the thrust, hence great care should be taken to see that the left arm is not deprived of its freedom of action by gripping the rifle too hard with the left hand.

POSITION OF GUARD

The Position of "Rest"

The feet are retained at the position of Guard. The piece is lowered and held in the easiest and most comfortable position.

The Position of High Port

Being at the position of Guard. Without changing the position of the hands on the piece, carry the rifle so that the left wrist is level with and directly in front of the left shoulder. The right hand is level with the belt.

Practice will be had at the position of *High Port* with the right hand quitting the piece, it being held approximately in position with the left hand alone. This will be found advantageous when jumping ditches, climbing out of trenches, surmounting obstacles, etc., leaving the right hand free.

The Position of Long Point

Being at the position of Guard. Thrust the point of the bayonet vigorously towards the point of the objective, to the full extent of the left arm, the stock running alongside of and kept close to the right inner fore arm. The body is inclined forward; left knee well bent; right leg braced, and weight of body pressed well forward with the sole of the right foot, heel raised. The chief power in the Point is derived from the right arm with the weight of the body behind it, the left arm and hand being employed to direct the point of the bayonet at the objective.

The eyes must be fixed on the objective. In making the point other than straight to the front the left foot will be moved laterally in the direction to which the point is made. After progress has been made in the execution of the simple point as indicated above, practice should include stepping forward with the rear foot when the assault is delivered.

The common faults in the execution of the Long Point will be noted as follows:

1. The rifle is drawn back slightly before delivering the point, which makes for a momentary loss of time that may give an opponent the advantage and should be assiduously guarded against.

2. The stock of the piece is held too high, which makes the guiding of the point of the bayonet with the left hand more difficult, and reduces accuracy in delivering the point at the exact spot intended.

3. The eyes are not directed on the point of the attack. This is an er-

THE LONG POINT

ror. One that may cause a man to miss his mark. The soldier must realise what this means in hand to hand fighting. The opponent will get him.

4. The left knee is not sufficiently bent, which does not allow the point to be made with the force intended.

5. The body is not thrust sufficiently forward, which reduces just that much the force of the attack.

6. The point is started at too great a distance from the objective to make a hit. Practice must be conducted in making the point until the soldier knows the exact distance at which he will have to start to produce the maximum effect. This distance is between four and five feet.

During the later stages of the instruction the men should also be taught to step forward with the rear foot when delivering the point.

THE WITHDRAWAL AFTER A LONG POINT

Being at the position of Long Point. To withdraw the bayonet. Draw the piece straight back until the right hand is well behind the hip. Immediately assume the position of Guard. If the leverage or proximity of the object transfixed with the bayonet renders it necessary, prior to the withdrawal, the left hand is slipped up close to the stacking swivel.

In the preliminary instruction all Points will be immediately followed by a withdrawal, prior to assuming the position of guard.

PROGRESSION

THE WITHDRAWAL

After the several positions hereinbefore described have been learned, the Points should be made at a definite place on a target, such as the throat, the stomach, the head, etc.

As progress is made, the pause between the point and the withdrawal is shortened until the soldier comes directly to the position of Guard from the point. Proficiency will finally be attained in making a "feint point" at one part of the target and the real point at another, for example: Feint at the head and point at the right thigh; feint at the stomach and point at the neck, etc.

Attacks at a retreating foe should be made against the kidneys, the position of which should be shown to the soldier.

VULNERABLE PARTS OF THE BODY

If possible, the point of the bayonet should be directed against the opponent's throat, especially in hand to hand fighting. The point of the bayonet will easily enter and make a fatal wound on penetrating a few inches. Other and more or less exposed parts are the face, chest, lower abdomen, thighs and the region of the kidneys when the back is turned. Four to six inches penetration is sufficient to incapacitate and allow for a quick withdrawal, whereas if a bayonet is driven home too far it is often impossible to withdraw it.

As soon as the nomenclature of the positions and movements are learned the men should work in pairs. They should be practiced in pointing in various directions. 1. At the opposite man's hand, which he places in various positions on and off the body. 2. At thrusting rings tied on the end of a stick.

This practice is conducted without word of command, so that the eyes and brain may be trained.

It is not sufficient that a dummy be merely transfixed. Some particular spot on the dummy should constitute the target. Discs or numbers should be placed on the dummy and the men required to point at a distance of about five feet from it and later as they become more proficient, to point after advancing several paces. The advance must be made in a practical manner and the point delivered with either foot to the front.

The rifle must never be drawn back when making a Long Point in a forward movement. The impetus of the body and the forward stretching of the arms supply sufficient force.

The bayonet must be withdrawn immediately after the Point has been delivered, and a forward threatening attitude assumed by the side of or beyond the dummy.

To guard against accidents the men must be at least five feet apart and the bayonet scabbard should be on the bayonet.

The principles of this practice should be observed when pointing at dummies in trenches, standing upright on the ground or suspended from gallows. They should be applied at first slowly and deliberately. No attempt must be made to carry out the Final Assault Practice until the men have been carefully instructed in and have thoroughly mastered the preliminary lessons.

LESSON NO. 2

THE PARRIES

Being at the position of Guard: The right or left parry is executed by vigorously straightening the left arm, without bending the wrist or twisting the rifle in the hand, and forcing the piece to the right or left far enough to fend off the adversary's weapon. The eyes must be kept on the weapon that is being parried and not on the eyes of the opponent as indicated in our bayonet combat training.

The common faults in the execution of the parries consist of:

1. Making a wide, sweeping parry, with no forward movement of the bayonet or body in it.

2. The eyes are taken off the weapon that is being parried.

The men should be taught to regard the parry as a part of an offensive movement, namely of the Point, which would immediately follow it in actual combat. For this reason, as soon as the movements of the parries have been learned they should always be accompanied by a slight forward movement of the body.

Parries will be practiced with the right as well as with the left foot forward, preparatory to the practice of parrying when advancing.

PRACTICE

Men when learning the parries should be required to observe the movements of the rifle carefully, and should not be kept longer at this practice than is necessary for them to understand what is required, that is vigorous, yet controlled action.

The men work in pairs with scabbards on the bayonets, one man pointing with the stick and the other parrying it. The position of guard is resumed after each parry. At first this practice must be slow and deliberate, without being allowed to become mechanical, and will be progressively increased in rapidity and vigour.

Later a point at that part of the body indicated by the opposite man's hand should immediately follow the parry, and, finally sticks long enough to represent the opponent's weapon at the position of guard should be attached to dummies and parried before delivering the point. (See Targets.)

The men must be taught to parry points made at them:

1. By an enemy in a trench when they are themselves on the parapet.

2. By an enemy on the parapet when they are on the trench.

3. When both are fighting on the same level at close quarters in a deep trench.

LESSON NO. 3

THE SHORT POINT

Being at the position of Guard: Shift the left hand quickly towards the muzzle and draw the rifle back to the full extent of the right arm, the butt either upwards or downwards, according as a low point or high point is to be made. Deliver the point vigorously to the full extent of the left arm.

The short point is used at a range of about three feet. In close fighting it is the natural point to make when the bayonet has just been withdrawn after a long point. If a strong withdrawal is necessary the right hand should be slipped above the back sight after the short point has been made.

By placing two discs on a dummy the short point should be taught in conjunction with the long point, the first disc being transfixed with the latter and the second with the former. On delivery of the long point if the left foot is forward, the short point would take place with the right foot forward and *vice versa.*

The parries should be practiced from the position of the short point.

LESSON NO. 4

THE JAB OR UPWARD POINT

Being at the position of Short Point: Shift the right hand up the rifle and grasp it above the balance, at the same time bringing the piece to an almost vertical position close to the body. From this position, bend the knees and jab the point of the bayonet upwards into the throat or under the chin of the opponent.

The common faults in this movement are:

147

THE SHORT POINT

1. The rifle is drawn backward and not held sufficiently upright.

2. The rifle is grasped too low with the right hand.

From the position of Jab, the men will be practiced in fending off an attack made on any part of their body by an opponent.

When making a Jab from the position of guard, the right, being the thrusting hand, will be brought up first.

The Jab can be employed successfully in close quarter fighting in narrow trenches or when embraced by an enemy.

METHODS OF INJURING AN OPPONENT

It should be impressed upon the soldier that, although a man's point has missed, or has been parried or his bayonet has been broken, he can, as attacker, still maintain his advantage by injuring his opponent in one of the following ways:

Butt Strike 1. Swing the butt up at the opponent's crotch, ribs, forearm, etc., using a half arm blow and advancing the rear foot.

This is essentially a half arm blow from the shoulder, keeping the elbow rigid. It can be executed only when the rifle is grasped at the small of the stock.

Butt Strike 2. If the opponent jumps back so that the first butt strike misses, the rifle will come into a horizontal position over the left shoulder, butt to the front. The attacker will then step in with the rear foot and dash the butt into his opponent's face.

Butt Strike 3. If the opponent retires still further out of distance, the attacker again closes up and slashes his bayonet down on his opponent's head or neck.

Butt Strike 4. If the point is beaten or brought down, the butt can be used effectively by crashing it down on the opponent's head with an over-arm blow, advancing the rear foot. When the opponent is out of distance Butt Strike 3 can again be used.

In individual fighting the butt can also be used horizontally against the opponent's ribs, forearm, etc. This method is impossible in trench fighting or in an attack, owing to the horizontal sweep of the bayonet to the attacker's left.

The men must be impressed with the fact that the butt must never be used when it is possible to use the point of the bayonet effectively.

Butt Strikes can be used only under certain conditions and in certain positions. If the soldier acquires absolute control of his weapon under these conditions, he will be able to adapt himself to all other phases of close in fighting. For example, when a man is gripped by an

THE JAB

opponent, so that neither the point nor the butt can be used, the knee brought up against the crotch or the heel stamped on the instep may momentarily disable him and make him release his hold. When wrestling the opponent may be tripped by forcing his weight on to one leg and then kicking that leg from under him. These methods will only temporarily disable an enemy, who must be killed with the bayonet.

PRACTICE

When the men have been shown the methods of using the butt and the knee, they should be practiced by affixing several discs on a dummy and executing combination exercises at them. For example, point at one disc, use the knee on another fixed low down, jab at a third, etc. For practice with the Butt, light dummies should be used to prevent injury to the piece.

TACTICAL APPLICATION OF THE BAYONET

A bayonet assault should preferably be made under cover of fire, or darkness or as a surprise. Under these circumstances the prospect of success is greatest, for a bayonet is useless at any range except in hand to hand fighting.

The bayonet is essentially a weapon of offense to be used with skill and vigour. To await an opportunity for using the bayonet entails defeat. An approaching enemy will simply stand out of bayonet range and shoot down the defenders.

In an assault the enemy should be killed with the bayonet. Firing should be avoided. A bullet passing through an opponent's body may kill a friend who happens to be in the line of fire.

THE BAYONET ASSAULT

Training in the final assault is conducted only after the soldier has received a thorough course of instruction in the preliminary lessons and has acquired complete control over his weapons. This training must approximate as nearly as possible the conditions of actual fighting. Instructors should endeavour by every means in their power to arouse the interest and imagination of the men. Each problem should be carefully explained beforehand so that every man may have a complete knowledge of just exactly what is being attempted. Each target must be regarded as an armed opponent and each line of targets as an enemy line, attacking, defending or retiring, to be disposed of accordingly.

Any tendency towards carelessness and slackness must be corrected at once and all the men must be impressed with the fact that a practice assault that is not carried out with quickness, vigour and determination is worse than useless.

Lack of imagination or lack of understanding of what is being attempted, leading to a violation of the principles of tactics in practice assaults against dummy targets, can only lead to disaster in a real assault against the enemy.

Nervous tension, due to the anticipation of an attack, the advance across the open and the final dash at the enemy all combine to tire an assaulting party. It is only by their physical fitness and superior skill with the bayonet that they can overcome a comparatively fresh foe.

Accuracy in directing the bayonet when moving rapidly or surmounting obstacles; a thrust of sufficient force to penetrate clothing and equipment; a clean withdrawal, which requires no small effort, especially when the bayonet is fixed by a bone; are all of the greatest importance.

Method of Carrying the Rifle with Bayonet Fixed

1. A quick, short advance. Carry the rifle at the position of "High Port." This position is suitable for close formations. It minimizes risks of accidents when surmounting obstacles. It can be maintained with the left hand alone, allowing a free use of the right when necessary.

2. Long advance, in close formation. Carry the rifle slung over the left shoulder, barrel perpendicular, sling to the front. This allows the free use of both hands.

3. Long advance, in open order. Carry the rifle at the "Trail."

Teamwork

The importance of teamwork, discipline, and organised control throughout the conduct of the bayonet assault cannot be too strongly impressed upon the men. In this, as well as in all other tactical operations, success can only be achieved through the closest cooperation of all concerned. While individual initiative is to be encouraged, it must be strictly subordinated to the will of the leader of the assaulting party. The failure of an enterprise can usually be traced to the lack of this close cooperation.

The Advance

1. All members of the attacking party must "go over the top," that is, leave the trench, or rise from cover simultaneously.

2. The first stage, especially of a long advance, is slow and steady—not faster than the pace of the slowest man.

Such an advance has a decided moral effect on the enemy. It will produce the maximum shock at the moment of impact. It allows the attacking force to reach its objective without undue exhaustion. On the other hand, if the assault is allowed to develop without control and in a haphazard fashion, the moral effect of the steady advance of a resistless wall of men is lost and the defenders will be given time to dispose of their opponents in detail.

THE CHARGE

The actual charge will not be delivered over a greater distance than 20 paces. Within the last ten paces the piece will be brought to the position of guard. The alignment will be maintained as far as possible until actual contact is gained.

As soon as a position is carried and prior to any further advance or any other operation whatsoever, the line must be reformed and every precaution taken against a counter attack. In Trench Warfare, the indiscriminate pursuit with the bayonet must never be permitted unless orders to that effect have been given by the leaders of the assaulting party. The attacking troops are not so fresh as the enemy and experience has shown that unorganised pursuit is exposed to ambuscades and machine gun fire. In most cases the work of immediate pursuit is better accomplished by the supporting artillery assisted by the rapid fire of the infantry on the retreating enemy.

ASSAULT PRACTICE

Throughout the period of training the men, the men should be constantly practiced in:

1. The recognised method of carrying the rifle with the bayonet fixed.

2. The rapid advance out of deep trenches.

3. Teamwork and control of advancing line. Fire discipline, direction and control.

4. The art of using the bayonet with effect in the cramped space of communication and fire trenches.

5. Reforming and opening fire after an assault.

6. Acting as leaders of an attacking party.

FINAL ASSAULT PRACTICE

One of the best methods of training a command in the final assault is to construct a section of trench, forming a course, over which the training may be conducted. The edges of the trenches should be pro-

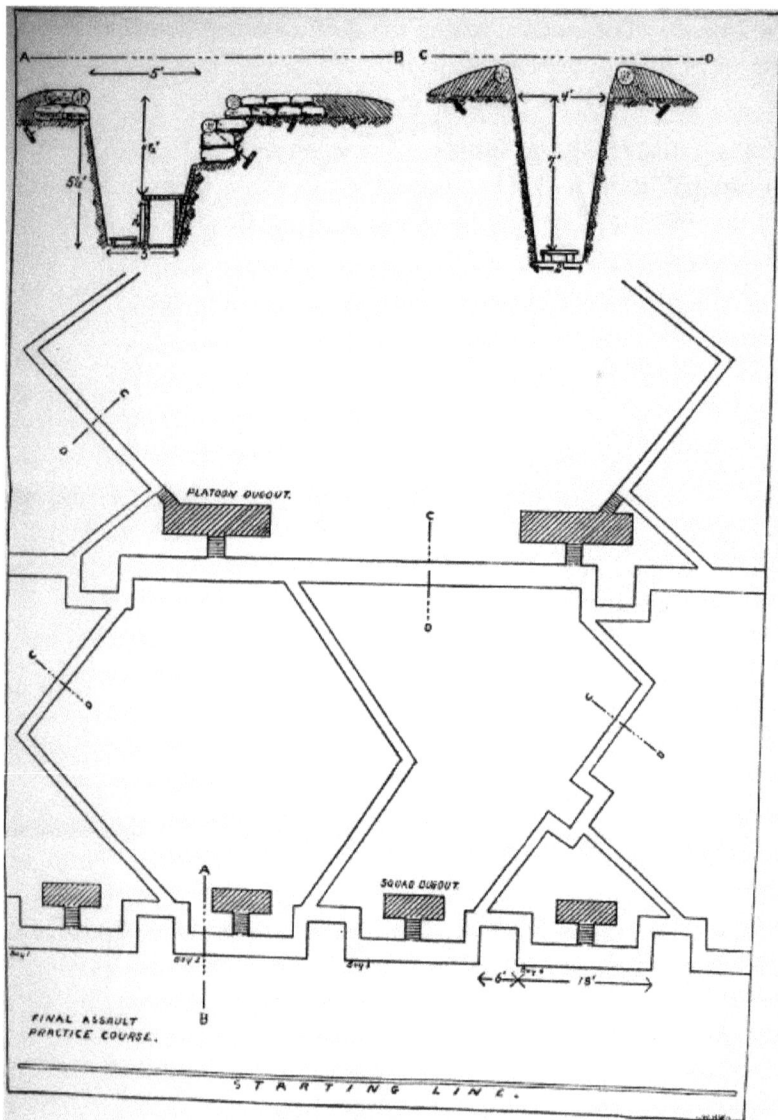

A ———————————————— B C ———————————————— D

5'

1'

1'6"

7'

5½'

3

2

PLATOON DUGOUT.

C

D

C

D

C

D

C

D

A

SQUAD DUGOUT.

6' · 5'4"

15'

FINAL ASSAULT
PRACTICE COURSE.

B

STARTING LINE.

tected by logs anchored back in the parapets or solid ground. Constant use will soon wear them down if this precaution is not taken. Cinders placed on the course are a great advantage, for they prevent the men from slipping.

When dummy targets are laid on the ground or on parapets, care should be taken to see that the earth under them is free from stones, otherwise bayonets will be injured when the thrust penetrates clear through the dummy and into the ground.

For this practice work it will be well to select the bayonets of the company that are most worn and use them exclusively.

Most interesting and practical problems in the tactics of trench warfare can be solved by combining the assault practice with other forms of training such as the operations of grenadier squads in clearing fire trenches and communication trenches; throwing hand grenades, to cover the assault; barricading with sandbags and the construction of trenches.

The illustration herein shows a type of Final Assault Practice course, that may be prepared with a minimum expenditure of labour and material. It occupies a space of about 100 feet in width and may be of varying depth according to the elements that it is desired to introduce. A platoon of four squads with the squad leaders taken out of the line and placed in rear to direct their squads, may be run over the course with safety after the men have had sufficient preliminary training. The elements of this course are:

1. A line of traversed type of fire trench. There being four bays, 18 feet long with 6 foot traverses. This trench is the simple type of standing trench shown in the profile.

2. A supervision trench located parallel to and about 50 feet in rear of the fire trench. Profile shown.

3. Communication zigzags from the supervision trench to the fire trench.

4. Two communication zigzags of three legs each running to the rear from the supervision trench.

5. The location of squad dugouts in rear of the bays of the fire trench and platoon dugouts just in rear of the supervision trench are indicated. It is not necessary for the purposes to excavate these. The location of the entrances in the trenches should be indicated.

The starting line is 40 feet in front of the traversed fire trench. This may be a deep trench or merely a line as desired. The trench gives good practice for the men in getting out of a fire trench, quickly and forming a line beyond. The whole system of trenches should be constructed on ground that can be easily drained.

1. Portable gallows for the suspension of from one to four targets are constructed and located at such points as may be desired in the area between the fire trench and the supervision trench and that to the rear of the latter.

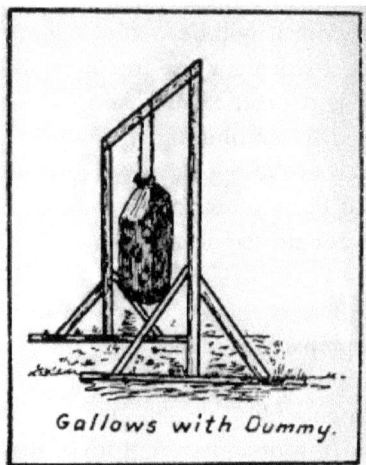

Gallows with Dummy.

2. Shell craters may be excavated in the open spaces mentioned above in which dummy targets may be placed.

3. Portable Turk's Head may be constructed and placed at such points as may be desired in the trenches or in the open spaces above ground.

4. Dummy targets may be placed wherever desired.

TARGETS

Target A. Consists of a portable gallows having one dummy target.

Target B. Consists of a portable gallows having two or more dummy targets.

Target C. Consists of a portable gallows the same as Target A, having a dummy target with the stick protruding to the front to represent the opponent's bayonet.

Target D. Consists of a dummy target to lie on the ground or rest against the side wall of the trench.

Target E. Is a Turk's Head.

156

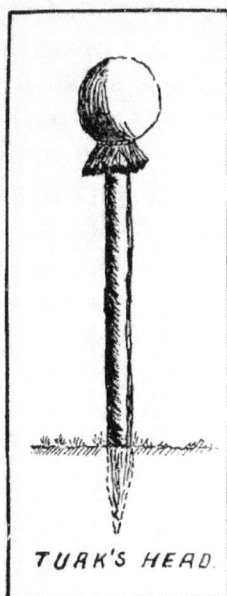

TURK'S HEAD.

Dummies
in Trenches.

Types of Dummies

CONSTRUCTION OF GALLOWS

The gallows for targets A, B, and C is constructed as shown in the plate. Two standards are made as indicated and joined together by pieces of 2x4 of the desired length at A and B. For Target A this length should be about 6 feet; for Target B at least 5 feet should be allowed for each dummy. Where more than two targets are hung the top cross piece had better be a 4x4 instead of a 2x4.

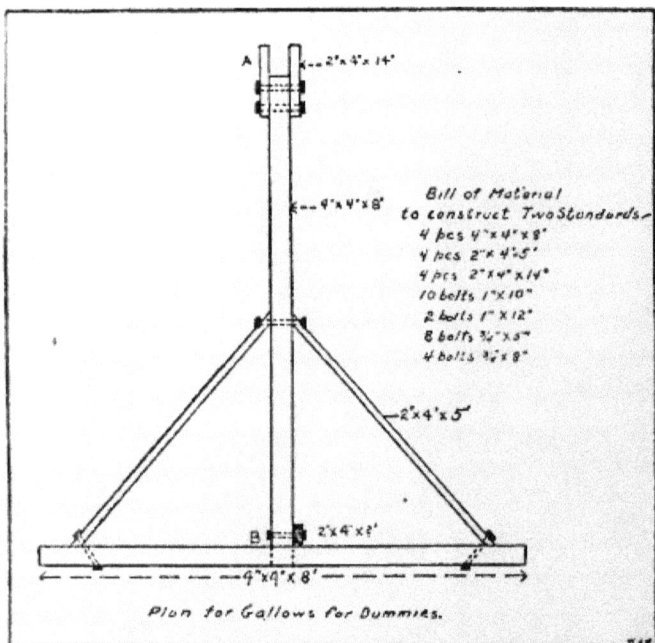

Plan for Gallows for Dummies.

CONSTRUCTION OF DUMMIES

The dummy may consist of a gunny sack filled with straw and packed tightly. It may be an old uniform stuffed with straw. A more elaborate form that tends to hold the bayonet when it is thrust into it may be made as follows:

1. Split a sack along the side and across the end forming a manta. Lay it on the ground.

2. Place a layer of straw about 20 inches wide and nearly the length of the sack, allowing a few inches at the top and bottom for folding over. Now place a layer of good stiff sod on the straw. Follow this with another layer of straw. Follow this of sod and straw until the dummy is 8 or 10 inches thick. Then put a one-quarter board with the grain up and down on top of the whole.

3. Fold in the sides and top tight and sew them together with a strong twine and a baling needle.

4. Run a strong rope around the outside edges, turning it at each corner to make a loop by which the dummy may be hanged to the gallows.

For those dummies that are to sit on the ground a piece of 2-inch plank placed across the bottom before the sacking is folded and sewed will form a good base. On these the rope will be omitted.

CONSTRUCTION OF "TURK'S HEAD"

On the end of a pole about six feet long place a ball of straw about 9 inches in diameter, packed tightly in gunny sacking. Sharpen the other end of the pole so that it may be stuck in the ground.

CONSTRUCTION OF PARRYING DUMMY TARGET

Take one of the ordinary dummies. Put a Turk's Head on a stick about 4 feet long and nail some canvas or gunny sacking to the other end so that the edges will spread out. Sew the canvas to a point on the dummy about two-thirds of the way down the front and suspend it from the top with strong ropes attached to the upper corners of the dummy.

DISCS ON TARGET

With a view to attaining accuracy in the points, cardboard discs about 3 inches in diameter should be placed on the front of the dummies. The soldier should not merely try to hit the dummy with his bayonet, but he should endeavour to make hits on the discs.

EXERCISES

The exercises that may be devised with this equipment are of an infinite variety, ranging from practice runs of one man to each bay of the trench, merely going into and out of the trenches, to an entire squad assaulting each bay with targets placed all along the course.

The following are suggested exercises:

EXERCISE 1

Number of men to make the run: Four, one at each bay.

Targets: No. l. One Target D, half exposed on parapet at the left corner of Bay 4 to represent a man firing over the parapet.

No. 2. One Target D, resting against the rear wall of the fire trench of Bay 4, at the opening of the dugout, to represent a man just emerging from the squad dugout.

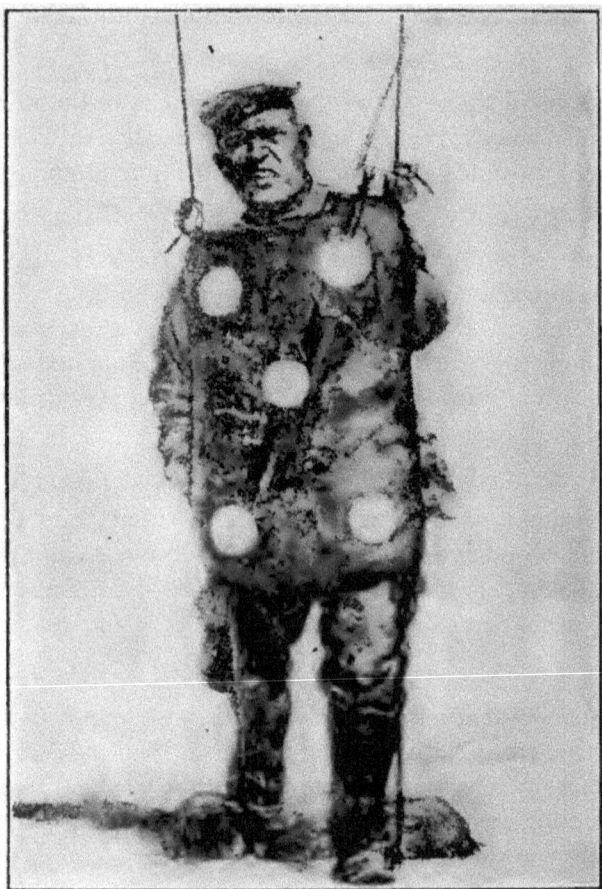

EACH DUMMY MUST BE REGARDED AS AN
ACTUAL ARMED OPPONENT

No. 3. One Target A, midway between the fire trench and the supervision trench.

No. 4. One Target E, in supervision trench.

No. 5. One Target D, in supervision trench at the entrance to the communication trench.

No. 6. One Target D, on the ground to the rear of the supervision trench. Note. Targets for the man making the run against Bay 4 are stated. Those for the other men making the run are similarly located.

THE RUN

The method of making the run will be explained for the man making the run at Bay 4. The other men proceed in a similar manner.

Being in the prone position at the starting point the soldier rises quickly to his feet and advances at the double time (not running) towards Target No. 1, the piece being carried at the "High Port." When within about 8 paces of Target No. 1 the piece is brought to the position of guard and when at the proper distance the target is attacked with a vigorous "Long Point." This is followed by a clean withdrawal.

The soldier then jumps into the fire trench and attacks Target No. 2 or attacks from over the fire trench as is desired. He then climbs out of the fire trench and continues his advance attacking Target No. 3 with a Long Point; No. 4 with a Long Point; No. 5 with a Short Point and No. 6 with a Long Point, each being followed by a clean withdrawal of the bayonet.

EXERCISE 2

Number of men to make run: Two squads, one at Bays 1 and 2, and the other at Bays 3 and 4.

Targets: The targets are given only for the four men making the run against Bay 4. Those for the other three bays are similarly arranged.

No. 1. Four Targets D, half exposed on parapet of bay to represent men firing over the parapet.

No. 2. Four Targets D, lying on ground or in shell crater a few feet in rear of the bay.

No. 3. Four Targets A or C, in the open area about midway between the fire trench and the supervision trench.

No. 4. Four Targets D in the bottom of the supervision trench.

No. 5. Four Targets E, a few yards in rear of the supervision trench.

The run is conducted in the same manner as explained for Exercise 1. Additional precautions will have to be taken to prevent the men from injuring one another with their bayonets.

The line attacks Target No. 1. The men jump over the fire trench landing on the parados and immediately attack Target No. 2. The line passes on towards Target No. 3, jumping all trenches encountered and attack Target No. 3 with a parry and a point if Target C is used and with a point if Target A is used. The line then goes into the supervision trench and attacks Target No. 4, climbing out immediately and advancing on Target No. 5 which is attacked by a "Jab."

In order to save time a second line may be started from the starting line when the first has passed beyond the fire trench and towards the supervision trench.

After the men have been taken through a thorough course of training in the individual instruction, problems should be devised in which a squad assaults a section of the trench system under the direction of the squad leader. This is followed by exercises conducted by the platoon leader, the strength of the platoon being as many squads as can be employed at one time on the front of the section of trench system available.

Bayonet Training Manual Used by the British Forces

Infantry Journal May, 1917

Preface

Training in the use of the bayonet is receiving much attention from all the combatant nations in Europe. The aim of the instruction is twofold:

1. To develop great alertness of mind, readiness of muscle, and habit of quick obedience to command.

2. To develop fighting spirit.

Physical drill and bayonet training go hand in hand and their drill periods follow each other. The physical drill consists of calisthenic exercises for fifteen or twenty minutes, followed by some game or exercise requiring great quickness of movement. To accomplish the aims of this training, especially the first named above, it is necessary to execute with snap the movements in the physical drill.

The following is from the latest British Training Manual (1916), which is based on their experience, and the forces are now being trained in accordance therewith.

CHAPTER 1

Introductory

To attack with the bayonet effectively requires *good direction, strength and quickness* during a state of wild excitement and probably physical exhaustion. The limit of the range of a bayonet is about five feet (measured from the opponent's eyes), but more often the killing is at close quarters, at a range of two feet or less, when troops are struggling *corps à corps* in trenches or darkness.

The bayonet is essentially an offensive weapon—go straight at an opponent with the point threatening his throat and deliver a thrust wherever an opening presents itself. If no opening is obvious, then create one by beating off the opponent's weapon or making a "feint thrust" in order to make him uncover himself.

Hand-to-hand fighting with the bayonet is individual, which means that a man must think and act for himself and rely on his own resources and skill; but, as in games, he must play as one of a team and not for himself alone. *In a bayonet assault all ranks go forward to kill or be killed, and only those who have developed skill and strength by constant training will be able to kill.*

The spirit of the bayonet must be inculcated into all ranks, so that they go forward with that aggressive determination and confidence of superiority, born of continual practice, without which a bayonet assault will not be effective.

The technical points of bayonet fighting are extremely few and simple: the essence of bayonet training, and continuity of practice.

An important point to be kept in mind in bayonet training is the development of the individual by teaching him to think and act for himself. The simplest means of attaining this is to make men use their brains and eyes to the fullest extent by carrying out the practices, so far as possible, without words of command. This procedure develops individuality and confidence. Alertness and rapidity are qualities to be developed also.

As technique of bayonet fighting is so simple, long detail is quite unnecessary and makes the work monotonous. All instructions should be carried out on common-sense lines. It should seldom be necessary to give the detail of a "thrust" or "parry" more than two or three times, after which the classes should acquire the correct positions by practice. For this reason, a drill should rarely last more than thirty minutes. It should be remembered that nothing kills interest so easily as monotony.

The spirit of the bayonet is to be inculcated by describing the special features of bayonet and hand-to-hand fighting. The men must learn to practise bayonet fighting in the spirit and with the enthusiasm which animate them when training for their games, and to look upon their instructor as a trainer and helper.

Interest in the work is to be created by explaining the reasons for the various positions, the method of handling the rifle and bayonet, and the uses of the thrusts. Questions should be put to the men to find out whether they understand these reasons. When men realise the object of their work, they naturally take a greater interest in it.

Progression in bayonet training is regulated by obtaining: first, correct positions and good direction; then, quickness. Strength is the outcome of continual practice.

In order to encourage dash and gradually to strengthen the leg muscles, from the commencement of their training, classes should be frequently practised in charging short distances.

All company officers and non-commissioned officers should be taught how to instruct in bayonet fighting, in order that they may be able to teach their men in this very important part of a soldier's training. It should have place in all training schedules, and in all rest periods in war time.

Sacks for dummies should be filled with vertical layers of straw and thin sods, leaves, shavings, etc., in such a way as to give the greatest resistance without injury to the bayonet. A realistic effect, necessitating a strong withdrawal, as if gripped by a bone, is obtained by inserting pieces of hard wood, ¼ inch thick (pieces of crating or boxes), between the stuffing and the sack on the side facing the attacker, and the grain must be vertical.

These sack dummies can be made to stand on end by fixing a wooden cross or star (two or three pieces of wood about two inches broad and ¾ inch thick nailed across one another) in the base of the sack before filling it. They can also be placed with good effect on

rough tripods or tied to improvised stools. Dummy sacks should be suspended from gallows and weighted or tethered to the ground from the bottom corners.

By the use of a little ingenuity an officer can readily represent the torso of an opponent in positions simulating actual conditions.

The greatest care should be taken that the object representing the opponent and its support should be incapable of injuring the bayonet or butt. Only light sticks (the parrying stick here referred to is shown in plates) must be used for parrying practice.

The chief causes of injury to the bayonet are: insufficient instruction in the bayonet training lessons; failure to withdraw the bayonet clear of the dummy before advancing; and placing the dummies on hard, unprepared ground.

For practising direction, there must always be an aiming mark on the dummy. Cardboard discs for this purpose are desirable. By continually changing the position of the mark, the "life" of the dummies is considerably prolonged.

In the absence of discs, five or six spots or numbers can be painted on the dummies as marks.

CHAPTER 2

Preliminary Bayonet Lessons

Intervals and distances will be taken as in Infantry Drill Regulations, except that in formations for bayonet exercises the men should be at least six paces apart in every direction. Classes should always work with bayonets fixed.

Before requiring soldiers to take a position or execute a movement for the first time, the instructor shows them the position, explaining essential points, and giving the reasons for them. Then show the position a second time, making the class observe each movement, so that from the very commencement of the bayonet training, a man is taught to use his eyes and brain. The class is then ordered to assume the position explained and shown. Pick out the man who shows the best position and let the class look at and copy him. Remember that his position may not be ideal, but it is more correct than those assumed by the remainder, who, being beginners, cannot distinguish the difference between a good position and an ideal one. Many instructors err by trying to get a class of beginners to idealise at once.

The recruit course consists of five lessons and the Final Assault Practice.

The men should be accustomed to wear the cartridge belt in the training, and packs may be required to be worn in efficiency tests. For the "thrust" and "parrying" exercises a light stick, 5 feet to 5 feet 6 inches long and ¾ to 1 inch in diameter, must be provided for every two men.

Half an hour a day, at least five days a week, should be devoted to the daily practice in bayonet fighting for trained soldiers. By this daily practice accuracy of direction, quickness, and strength are developed, and a soldier is accustomed to using the bayonet under conditions which approximate to actual fighting. This half-hour should be apportioned to (1) thrusting at the body; (2) thrusting at paper balls on light sticks

at varying distances and directions; (3) parrying light sticks; (4) dummy work; and, when sufficiently proficient, (5) the final assault practice.

LESSON 1

Point of the bayonet directed at the base of the opponent's throat, the rifle held easily and naturally with both hands, the barrel inclined slightly (about 30 degrees) to the left, the right hand at the height of the belt grasping the small of the stock, the left hand holding the rifle at the most convenient position in front of the rear sight, so that the left arm is only slightly bent; *i.e.*, making an angle of about 150 degrees. The legs well separated in a natural position, such as a man walking might adopt on meeting with resistance; *i.e.*, left knee slightly bent, right foot flat on the ground, with toe inclined to the right front.

The position should not be constrained in any way, but be one of aggression, alertness, and readiness to go forward for immediate attack (see Plate 1).

COMMON FAULTS.

1. Leaning body back.
2. Left arm too much bent.
3. Right hand held too low and too far back.
4. Rifle grasped too rigidly, restraining all freedom of movement.
Assume the "order" in the easiest way without moving the feet.

"High port." In this position the hands hold the rifle as in guard; the left wrist level with, and directly in front of, the left shoulder; the right hand above the right groin and on level with the belt.

When jumping ditches, surmounting obstacles, etc., this position of the rifle should be approximately maintained with the left hand alone, leaving the right hand free.

Being in the position of *guard*, to execute "long thrust," grasp the rifle firmly, vigorously deliver the thrust to the full extent of the left arm, butt running alongside and kept close to the right forearm; body inclined forward; left knee well bent; right leg braced, and weight of the body pressed well forward, with the fore part of the right foot, heel raised.

The chief power in a thrust is derived from the right arm with the weight of the body behind it, the left arm being used more to direct the point of the bayonet. The eye must be fixed on the object thrust at. In making thrusts other than straight to the front, the left foot should move in the same direction as that in which the thrust is made. Dur-

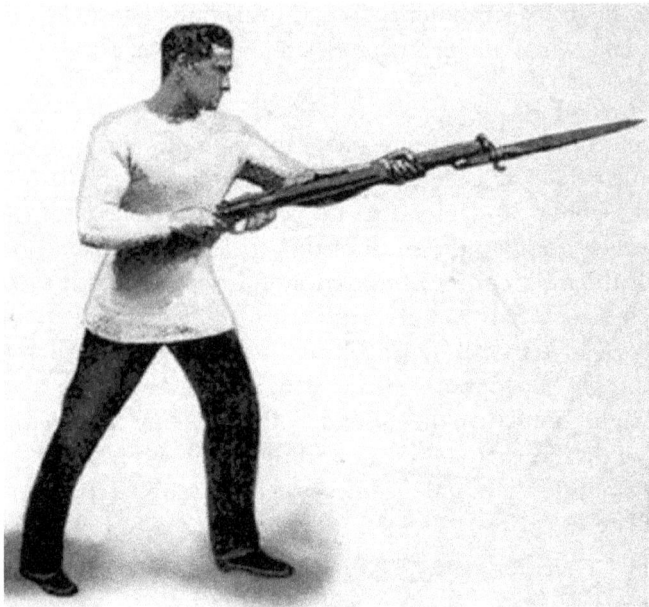

PLATE 1.—"GUARD."

PLATE 2—"LONG THRUST."

ing the later stages of this lesson the men should be practised in step-ping forward with the rear foot when delivering the thrust.

COMMON FAULTS.

1. Rifle drawn back before delivering the thrust.
2. Butt of the rifle held as high as or against the right shoulder.
3. The eyes not directed on the object.
4. Left knee not sufficiently bent.
5. Body not thrust sufficiently forward.

REMARKS.

The "long thrust" is made against an opponent at a range of about four to five feet from the attacker's eye.

To withdraw the bayonet after a long thrust has been delivered, draw the rifle straight back until the right hand is well behind the hip and immediately resume the guard. If the leverage or proximity to the object transfixed renders it necessary, the left hand must first be slipped up close to the stacking swivel and, when a pupil has reached that stage of delivering a thrust while advancing on a dummy, he will adopt this method.

After every thrust a rapid "withdrawal," essential to quick work with the bayonet, should be practised before returning to the guard.

PLATE 3—"WITHDRAWAL."

First Practice:

Men should always be made to thrust at a target, *e.g.*, at a named part of the body of the opposite man—"At the right eye; thrust, withdraw." Oblique thrust should be practised by thrusting at the men to the right or left fronts.

As progress is attained, the pause between the thrust and the withdrawal should be shortened, until the men reach the stage when they withdraw and come to guard directly after making the thrust, judging their own time. They should be taught to thrust at two or more parts of the body.

To practise action against a retreating foe, first show the position of the kidneys (small of back, either side of the spine).

If possible, the point of the bayonet should be directed against an opponent's throat, especially in hand-to-hand fighting. Other vulnerable and usually exposed parts are on the face, chest, lower abdomen, and thighs, and the region of the kidneys when the back is turned.

Four or six inches penetration is sufficient to incapacitate and allow for a quick withdrawal, whereas if a bayonet is driven home too far, it is often impossible to withdraw it. In such cases, a round should be fired to break the obstruction.

Second Practice:

The class working in pairs, with the instructor supervising, should be practised in thrusting in various directions: (1) at the opposite man's hand, which he places in various positions on and off his body; (2) at thrusting rings, or balls of paper, tied to the end of sticks (see Plates 6, 7, 8). This practice should be done without the word of command, so that the eye and brain may be trained.

Third Practice:

The men will be taught to transfix a disc or number painted on a dummy; first at a distance of about five feet from the dummy, *i.e.*, the extreme range of the bayonet; then, after advancing three or more paces. The advance must be made in the most practical and natural way, and should be practised with either foot to the front when the thrust is delivered. The rifle must never be drawn back when making a long thrust in a forward movement. The impetus of the body and the forward stretching of the arms supply sufficient force.

The bayonet must be withdrawn immediately after the thrust has been delivered, and a forward threatening attitude be assumed to the side or beyond the dummy.

Unless the rifle is firmly gripped, it is liable to injure the hand.

To guard against accidents, the men must be at least five feet apart when the practice is carried out collectively.

The principles of this practice will be observed when thrusting at dummies in trenches, standing upright on the ground or suspended on gallows. They should be applied at first slowly and deliberately, for *no attempt must be made to carry out the final assault practice before the men have been carefully instructed in, and have thoroughly mastered, the preliminary lessons.*

Lesson 2

The Right and Left Parry.

From the position of guard, vigorously straighten the left arm, without bending the wrist or twisting the rifle in the hand, and force the rifle forward far enough to the right (left) to ward off the adversary's weapon.

The eyes must be kept on the weapon which is being parried.

Common Faults.

1. Wide sweeping parry with no forward movement in it.
2. Eyes taken off the weapon to be parried.

Men must be taught to regard the parry as part of an offensive movement; namely, of the thrust which would immediately follow it in actual combat. For this reason, as soon as the movements of the parries have been learned, they should always be accompanied with a slight forward movement of the body.

Parries will be practised with right, as well as with the left, foot forward, preparatory to the practice of parrying when advancing.

First Practice:

Men learning the parries should be made to observe the movements of the rifle carefully, and should not be kept longer at this practice than is necessary for them to understand what is required—that is, vigorous yet controlled action.

Second Practice:

The class works in pairs with scabbards on the bayonets, one man thrusting with a stick and the other parrying; the guard is resumed after each parry. At first, this practice must be slow and deliberate, without being allowed to become mechanical, and will be progressively increased in rapidity and vigour. Later a thrust at that part of the body indicated by the opposite man's hand should immediately follow the parry, and, finally, sticks long enough to represent the opponent's weapon in the position of guard should be attached to the dummies and parried before delivering the thrust.

The men must be taught also to parry thrusts made at them: (1) by an opponent in a trench, when they are themselves on the parapet; (2) by an opponent on the parapet, when they are in the trench; and (3) when both are on the same level fighting at close quarters in a deep trench.

LESSON 3

To Execute the Short Thrust.

Shift the left hand quickly towards the muzzle and draw the rifle back to the full extent of the right arm, the butt either upwards or downwards as a low or a high thrust is to be made, then deliver the thrust vigorously to the full extent of the left arm.

The short thrust is used at a range of about three feet, and, in close fighting, it is the natural thrust to make when the bayonet has just been withdrawn after a long thrust. If a strong withdrawal is necessary, the right hand should be slipped above the rear sight after the short thrust has been made.

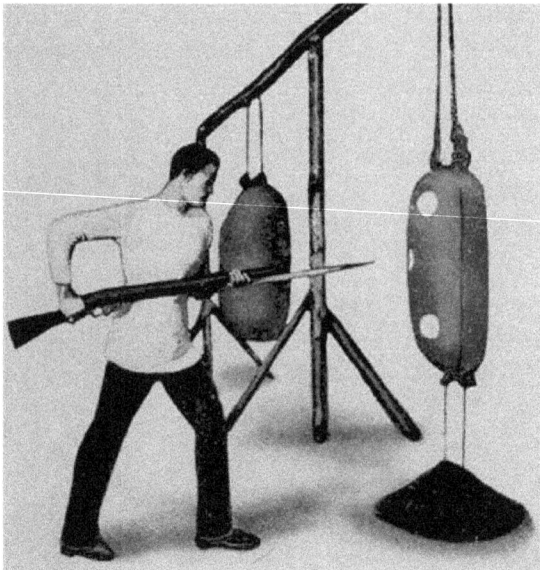

PLATE 4—"SHORT THRUST."

176

Practice:

The principles of the three practices of Lesson 1 should be observed so far as they apply. By placing two discs on a dummy, the short thrust should be taught in conjunction with the long thrust, the first disc being transfixed with the latter, the second disc with the former. On delivery of the long thrust, if the left foot is forward, the short thrust would take place with the right foot forward, and *vice versa*.

Parries will be practised from the position of the short thrust.

LESSON 4

The Jab or Upward Thrust.

From the position of short thrust shift the right hand up the rifle and grasp it above the rear sight, at same time bringing the rifle to an almost vertical position close to the body, and, from this position, bend the knees and jab the point of the bayonet upwards into the throat or under the chin of the opponent.

PLATE 5—"JAB."

Common Faults.

1. Rifle drawn backward and not held vertically enough.
2. Rifle grasped too low with the right hand.

From the jab position men will be practised in fending off an attack made on any part of them by an opponent.

PLATE 6—"JAB" AT THRUSTING RING.

When making a jab from the guard, the right, being in the thrusting hand, will be brought up first.

The jab can be employed successfully in close-quarter fighting in narrow trenches and when embraced by an opponent.

LESSON 5

Methods of Injuring an Opponent.

It should be impressed upon the class that, although a man's thrust has missed or has been parried or his bayonet has been broken, he can, as attacker, still maintain his advantage by injuring his opponent in one of the following ways:

Butt Stroke 1:

Swing the butt up at the opponent's crotch, ribs, forearm, etc., using a half-arm blow or advancing the rear foot.

PLATE 7—"BUTT STROKE 1."

Butt Stroke 2:

If the opponent jumps back so that the first butt stroke misses, the rifle will come into horizontal position over the left shoulder, butt leading; the attacker will then step in with the rear foot and dash the butt into his opponent's face.

Butt Stroke 3:

If the opponent retires still farther out of distance, the attacker again closes up and slashes his bayonet down on his opponent's head or neck.

Butt Stroke 4

If the thrust has been parried, the butt can be used effectively by crashing it down on the opponent's head with an over-arm blow, advancing the rear foot. When the opponent is out of distance, Butt Stroke 3 can again be used.

In individual fighting, the butt can also be used horizontally against the opponent's ribs, forearm, etc. This method is impossible in trench fighting or in an attack, owing to the horizontal sweep of the bayonet to the attacker's left.

PLATE 8—"BUTT STROKE 4."

It should be clearly understood that the butt must not be employed when it is possible to use the bayonet effectively.

Butt Stroke 1 is essentially a half-arm blow from the shoulder, keeping the elbow rigid, and it can therefore be successfully employed only when the right hand is grasping the rifle at the small of the butt.

Butt strokes can be used only in certain circumstances and positions, but if men acquire absolute control of their weapons under these conditions, they will be able to adapt themselves to all other phases of in-fighting. For instance, when a man is gripped by an opponent so that neither the thrust nor the butt can be used, the knee brought up against the crotch or the heel stamped on the instep may momentarily disable him and make him release his hold.

When wrestling, the opponent can be tripped by forcing his weight on to one leg and kicking that leg away from under him, or any other wrestler's trip; *e.g.*, "back heel."

The above methods will only temporarily disable an enemy, who must be killed with the bayonet, etc.

Practice:

When the classes have been shown the methods of using the butt and the knees, they should be practised on the padded stick; *e.g.*, fix several discs on a dummy; make a thrust at one; use the knee on another, low down; jab a third, and so on.

Light but still sufficiently-strong dummies should be used for practice with the butt, in order to avoid damage to it.

It is apparent that bayonet fighting as taught for trench warfare abroad lacks all the niceties of the art of bayonet fencing prescribed in our manual. *In bayonet fighting no "fouls" are known. The only rule to follow is: "Get after your man, put him out of action by any means at your command."*

CHAPTER 3

The Tactical Application of the Bayonet

A bayonet assault should preferably be made under cover of fire, surprise, or darkness. In these circumstances, the prospect of success is greatest, for a bayonet is useless at any range except hand-to-hand.

At night, all these covers can be utilised.

On the other hand, confusion is inherent in fighting by night, consequently the execution of a successful night attack with the bayonet requires considerable and lengthy training. Units should be frequently practised in night work with the bayonet.

The bayonet is essentially a weapon of offense, which must be used with skill and vigour, otherwise it has but little effect. To await passively an opportunity of using the bayonet entails defeat, since an approaching enemy will merely stand out of bayonet range and shoot down the defenders.

In an assault, the enemy should be killed with the bayonet. Firing should be avoided, for in the mix-up a bullet, after passing through an opponent's body, may kill a friend who happens to be in the line of fire.

FINAL ASSAULT PRACTICE.

This practice is to be carried out only after the men have been thoroughly trained in all the preliminary lessons and have acquired complete control of their weapons, otherwise injury to rifles and bayonets will result from improper application of the methods laid down in the foregoing instruction.

The Final Assault Practice must approximate as nearly as possible to the conditions of actual fighting.

Nervous tension, due to the anticipation of an attack, reacting on the body, as well as the dash across the open and the final dash at the enemy, combine to tire an assaulting party. It is only by their physical fitness and superior skill in the use of the bayonet that they can over-

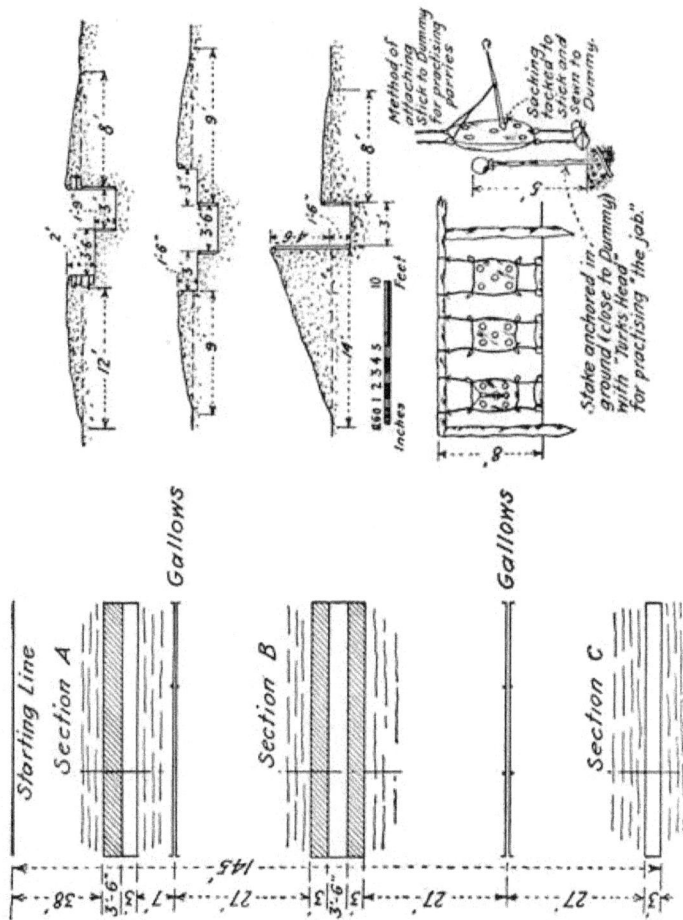

PLATE 8A.—Type of Simple "Final Assault Practice" Course.
It is attacked both ways, and the positions of the trench sack dummies are varied.

come a comparatively fresh foe.

Therefore, quick aim and good direction of the bayonet when moving rapidly or even when surmounting obstacles, accurate delivery of a thrust and sufficient strength and vigour to penetrate clothing and equipment, the clean withdrawal of the bayonet—which requires no small effort, especially should it be fixed by the bone—are of the greatest importance, and need the same careful attention and constant practice as are devoted to obtaining efficiency with the rifle.

In the Final Assault Practice, the charge brings the men to the first trench in a fairly exhausted condition, and the accuracy of the aim is tested by the disc, which can be perforated only by a true and vigorous thrust and a clean withdrawal.

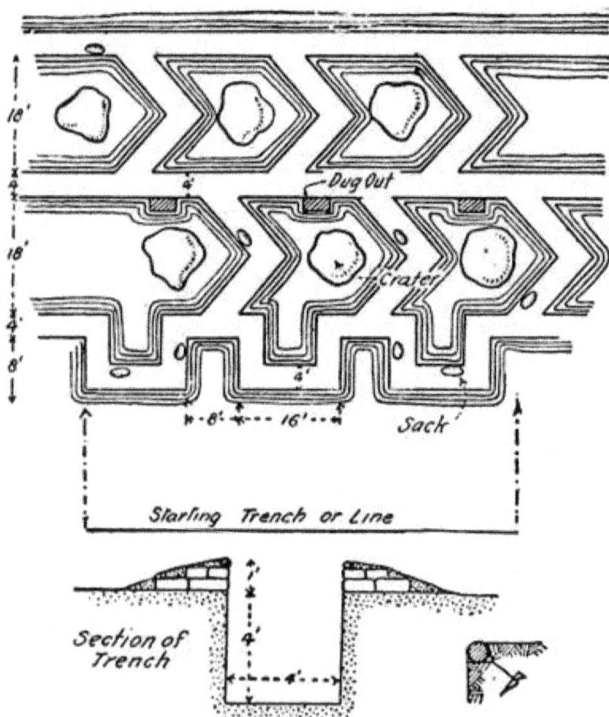

PLATE 8B.—EXAMPLE OF SHORT COMMUNICATION TRENCHES.
Which should form part of the usual Final Assault Practice Course, where, owing to the lack of ground, a "labyrinth" for daily practice with the bayonet in the confined space of a trench cannot be constructed within a convenient distance. On arrival in France drafts are tested in trench bayonet work.

For this practice, the men should be made to begin the assault from a trench six to seven feet deep, as well as from the open, and they should not cheer until close up to the enemy.

A reproduction of a labyrinth of trenches with dummies in the dugouts, and shelters between the trenches, forms an excellent Final Assault Practice Course. Assaults should be made from all four sides, in order to give variety. The edges of the trenches should be riveted, otherwise constant use will soon wear them out. Cinders scattered over the course prevent the men from slipping. If gallows cannot be erected, sack dummies should be placed on tripods or on end, as well as lying in trenches, or on parapets, with soft earth free from stones under them. The number, length, and construction of trenches are regulated by the available ground and by the ingenuity of the instructors.

Extremely interesting and practical schemes in trench warfare can be arranged by combining the Final Assault Practice with other branches of training; e.g., bombing, laying sand-bags, entrenching.

Competitions can be arranged by allotting marks for: (1) number of discs transfixed and carried on a bayonet; (2) time taken for signal to charge until the last man of the team passes the finishing post; and (3) form.

Competitions should never be carried out until the men have completed their lessons in bayonet training and thoroughly mastered the handling of the bayonet in the Final Assault Practice.

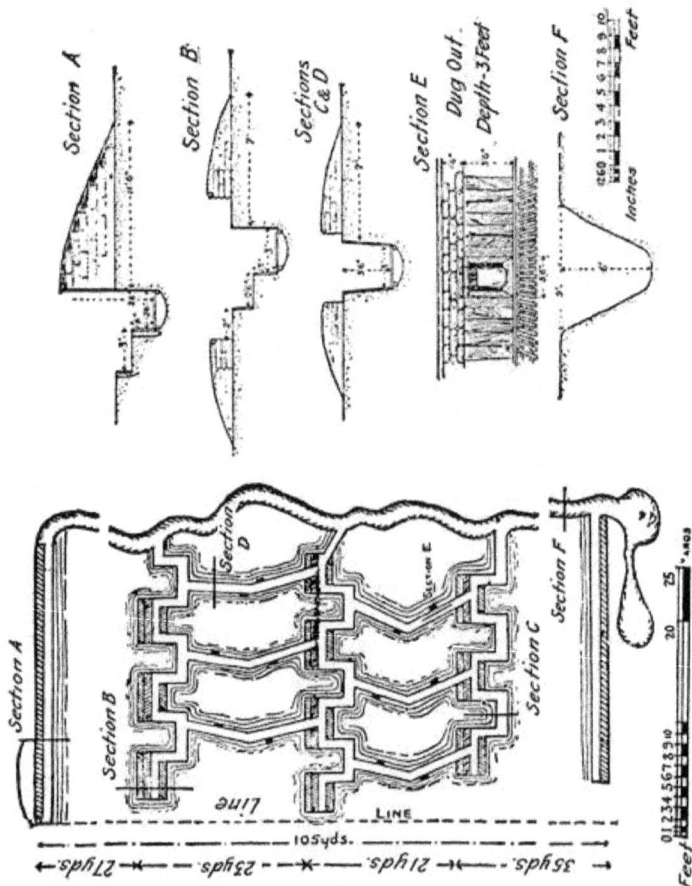

PLATE 8C.—TYPE OF "NURSERY" LABYRINTH.

The positions of the sack dummies are frequently changed: containing dummies, and the men practised in clearing such. The ground between the trenches is pitted with "craters" "cramped" grounds as well as in clearing the trenches.

CHAPTER 4

Tactical Principles to be Observed During Bayonet Training

METHOD OF CARRYING RIFLE WITH BAYONET FIXED.

Quick Short Advance (in the Open).

The rifle will be held at the "High Port." This position is suitable for close formation, minimises risk of accidents when surmounting obstacles, and can be maintained with the left hand alone, allowing free use of the right when necessary.

Long Advance (Close Formation).

The rifle will be slung over the left shoulder, sling to the front and perpendicular to the ground. This is a safe method of carrying the rifle and allowing the free use of both hands.

Long Advance (Open Order).

The rifle will be carried at the trail.

THE ASSAULT.

The importance of discipline and organised control throughout the conduct of a bayonet assault cannot be over-emphasised. It must be remembered that in this, as in all other military operations, success can be achieved only through the closest cooperation of all concerned; and that, while individual initiative is not to be discouraged, it must be strictly subordinated to the intention of the leader of the assaulting party.

Men should be shown by demonstration that it is in their own interests to pay attention to this point, and that the failure of an enterprise can usually be traced to the lack of this close cooperation.

During training, the following general principles will be observed:

1. All members of the attacking party must leave the trench or rise

from cover simultaneously. In addition to the advantages of surprise, needless casualties are thereby avoided.

2. The first stage, especially of a long advance, will be slow and steady—not faster than the pace of the slowest man. Such an advance has a decided moral effect on the enemy, makes certain of the maximum shock at the moment of impact, and at the same time allows the attacking force to reach its objective without undue exhaustion. On the other hand, if the assault is allowed to develop without control and in a haphazard fashion, the moral effect of a steady, resistless wall of men is lost, and the defenders may be given time to dispose of their opponents in detail.

Bayonet control in the attack is just as important and fully as practicable as fire control, and it depends altogether on discipline, which must be taught by close-order work, and on thorough technical instruction in the use of the bayonet. Tactical bayonet control will then follow without much difficulty, provided the instructor has done his work properly.

The actual charge will not be made over a greater distance than twenty paces. Within the last ten yards, and before closing with the enemy, the rifle will be brought to the threatening, yet defensive, guard position. Line will, as far as possible, be maintained until actual contact with the enemy is gained.

As soon as the enemy's position has been carried, and prior to any attack on a further position, or any other operation whatsoever, every precaution must be taken against a counter-attack. In trench warfare, indiscriminate pursuit with the bayonet must never be allowed unless orders to that effect have been given by the leader of the assaulting party. The attacking troops are not so fresh as the enemy, and experience has shown that unorganised pursuit lends itself to ambush and casualties from machine-gun fire. In most cases the work of immediate pursuit is better done by the supporting artillery, the infantry assisting by rapid fire on the retreating enemy.

Assault Practice.

A useful form of Final Assault Practice which can be adapted to a variety of combat exercises is described in following paragraphs. The following materials are assumed:

"A." Communicating trenches leading to a fire trench with an open space in front.

"B." An occupied enemy-trench.

"C." Gallows with dummies, representing the enemy.

    (1) retiring from "B" or

    (2) coming up in support of "B" or

    (3) making a counter-attack on the captured trench "B."

PLATE 9—EACH DUMMY MUST BE REGARDED
AS AN ACTUAL ARMED OPPONENT.

1. The attacking party makes a controlled assault on "A," which is cleared of the enemy.

2. It then re-formed and an assault is launched on "B," after taking which

3. "C" is regarded in one or other of the above ways, and action taken accordingly.

Throughout the training, men must be constantly practised in:

1. The recognised method of carrying the rifle with bayonet fixed.

2. Rapid advance out of deep trenches.

3. Control and maintenance of line and opening fire during an advance.

4. Using the bayonet with effect in the cramped space of communicating and fire trenches.

5. Re-forming and opening of fire after the assault.

6. Acting as leaders of attacking party.

Instructors should endeavour by every means in their power to arouse the interest and imagination of their men during the assault practice. The special phase of the combat which is to be carried out in the exercise should invariably be explained beforehand. Each dummy must be regarded as an actual armed opponent, and each line of dummies as an enemy line attacking, defending, or retiring, and be disposed of accordingly.

Any tendency toward carelessness or slackness must be instantly checked, and it should be impressed on all ranks that a practice assault which is not carried out with the necessary quickness, vigour, and determination is worse than useless.

Lack of imagination, which allows men and their leaders to violate the most elementary principles of tactics in practice assaults against dummies, can lead only to disaster in a real assault against an enemy.

CHAPTER 5

General Instructions for Bayonet Training Practice

1. "Guard," "withdrawals," "thrusts," "parries," and the "jab" will be taught first with the left, then with the right foot forward.

2. The position from which the "short thrust" is made is shown in Plate IV. All short thrusts will be practised from this position. Except after a thrust into a dummy, make a momentary pause in this position so as to break men of the habit of drawing back the rifle from the guard before making the thrust.

3. From the outset squads will be frequently practised in charging for short distances in the open as a strengthening exercise for the legs and a quickening exercise.

4. A target at which to thrust will always be named when working by word of command; it will be indicated by the position of hand when working in class and be clearly marked on all dummies.

5. When working in ranks, the distance apart must be sufficient to avoid all danger of accident when the thrusts are being made. When thrusts have been made advancing, the ranks will change position by coming to the high port, doubling past each other right shoulder to right shoulder and turning about. When working against dummies, men will always continue the movement past the dummy, which they will leave on their right.

6. The "withdrawal," once taught, will be made after each thrust. After a thrust advancing rear foot or on the advance, the hand will always be moved up the rifle, but in the first and second practices, since the arm and body are already stretched to their full extent, and the left hand cannot move farther forward, the hand will be shifted after the withdrawal from the long thrust.

7. All sticks must be padded at one end.

8. In the third practice, the thrusts will also be practised deliberately and progressively on dummies placed, as a preparation for the Final Assault Course, in positions of increasing difficulty; *e.g.*, on parapets and steps of shallow trenches, and in fire and communicating trenches.

9. Scabbards will not be removed from the bayonet except for thrusting at dummies.

CHAPTER 6

Progressive Program of Instruction

1. Intervals, distances, positions.

2. Explain hand-to-hand fighting, and inculcate the spirit of the bayonet.

LESSON 1.

3. Guard.

4. Order.

5. High Port.

First practice (in class, by word of command).

6. "Long thrust."

7. "Withdrawal" (*a*) after stationary thrust, (*b*) after thrust, advancing rear foot (Plate 3) (first demonstrated by instructor on a dummy).

8. Oblique long thrust.

9. Long thrust, followed by long thrust advancing rear foot.

10. Vulnerable spots explained; region of kidney shown; class practised in making thrusts at these.

Second practice (class working by eye):

11. Long thrust.

12. Long thrust, followed by long thrust advancing rear foot.

13. Varied direct and oblique long thrusts at thrusting ring.

Third practice (thrusting at dummy):

14. Long thrust (Plate 2).

15. Long thrust advancing rear foot.

16. Advancing long thrust.

17. Advance long thrust (at two or more dummies).

Lesson 2.

18. Explain value of parries; how, in charging, the parry must be strong enough to beat aside opponent's weapon.

First practice (in class, by word of command):

19. Explain, and make the class perform, the movements required for the various parries.

Second practice (class working by eye):

20. Parry stick pointed at the breast.

21. Parry stick pointed at the breast and deliver thrust.

22. Parry stick pointed at head, body, or legs.

23. Parry stick pointed in varying order at head, body, or legs, and deliver thrust.

24. When standing in a trench, parry a thrust made with stick from above.

25. When standing on a parapet, parry a thrust made with stick by a man in trench.

26. With stick parry a thrust made with stick by advancing opponent.

27. With stick parry a thrust made with stick by advancing opponent and come back with a thrust.

28. With stick parry thrust made with stick lightly held in one hand by charging opponent. (By holding his stick in right or left hand the attacker will clearly show on which side he is thrusting, and he will pass on that flank.)

Third practice (pointing at dummy with stick representing opponent's weapon):

29. Advance, parry stick, and thrust.

Lesson 3

30. Demonstrate the short thrust and explain when it is used (Plate 5).

First practice (in class, by word of command):

31. Short thrust.

32. Withdrawal: (*a*) stationary; (*b*) advancing rear foot. (Demonstrated by instructor on dummy.)

33. Oblique short thrust.

34. Short point advancing rear foot.

35. Long thrust advancing rear foot, followed by short thrust advancing rear foot.

Second practice (class working by eye):

36. Short thrust.

37. Short thrust advancing rear foot.

38. Long thrust advancing rear foot, followed by short thrust advancing rear foot.

39. Varied direct and oblique long and short thrusts at thrusting ring.

40. Practise various parries, parries and thrusts, from short thrust position (Plate 4).

Third practice (thrusting at dummy):

41. Short thrust.

42. Short thrust advancing rear foot.

43. Long thrust advancing rear foot; short thrust advancing rear foot.

44. Advance, long thrust, short thrust (at two dummies in suitable positions).

Lesson 4

45. Demonstrate jab at dummy; then, by placing men of the squad in suitable positions, explain when and how it is used in conjunction with thrusts (Plate 5).

First practice (in class, by word of command):

46. Jab from jab position.

47. Short thrust advancing rear foot, jab advancing rear foot.

48. Long thrust advancing rear foot, jab advancing rear foot.

49. Long thrust advancing rear foot, short thrust advancing rear foot, jab advancing rear foot.

50. Short thrust advancing rear foot, jab advancing rear foot, long thrust advancing rear foot.

Second practice (class working by eye):

51. Jab at thrusting ring (Plate 6).

52. Direct and oblique long and short thrusts, and jabs in varying order at thrusting ring.

53. When in jab position, ward off high and low thrusts made with stick.

Third practice (thrusting at dummy):

54. Jab from jab position.

55. Short thrust advancing rear foot, and jab advancing rear foot.

56. Long thrust advancing rear foot, short thrust advancing rear foot, and jab advancing rear foot (at dummies).

57. Advance, long thrust, and jab.

58. Advance, long thrust, short thrust, and two or more jabs (at dummies).

Lesson 5

First practice (word of command):

59. Practise Butt Stroke 1.

60. Practise Butt Stroke 2.

61. Practise Butt Stroke 3.

62. Practise Butt Stroke 4.

Second practice (working by eye):

63. Butt Stroke 1 at padded stick (Plate 8).

64. Butt Stroke 2 at padded stick.

65. Butt Stroke 3 at padded stick.

66. Butt Stroke 4 at padded stick (Plate 8).

68. Long thrusts, short thrusts, and jabs at thrusting ring, with butt strokes at padded stick, varied.

69. Trips practised by men working in pairs.

Third practice (on dummy):

70. Thrust, jab, etc., at dummies, followed by Butt Strokes 1-4 at light dummies, and introducing kicks and any other form of in-fighting.

CHAPTER 7

A Guide for the Trained Soldier's Daily Practice

(30 Minutes.)

(1) 5 minutes.

(*a*) Long thrust at hand (11-12 Progressive Program of Instruction) (not more than 8 thrusts each man).

(*b*) Short thrusts (36, 37, 38, Progressive Program of Instruction) (not more than 10 thrusts each man).

(2) 5 minutes, steady advance over obstacles and charge 20 yards, about 100 yards in all.

(3) 4 minutes, parrying stick and thrusting (23, Progressive Program of Instruction).

(4) 4 minutes, butt strokes, each stroke twice (59, 60, 61, 62, Progressive Program of Instruction) or practise trips, etc. (69, Progressive Program of Instruction.)

(5) 6 minutes, long thrusts, short thrusts and jabs at thrusting ring, with butt strokes at pad stick, varied (68, Progressive Program of Instruction).

(6) 6 minutes, Final Assault Practice.

LEONAUR

ALSO FROM LEONAUR
AVAILABLE IN SOFTCOVER OR HARDCOVER WITH DUST JACKET

ESCAPE FROM THE FRENCH *by Edward Boys*—A Young Royal Navy Midshipman's Adventures During the Napoleonic War.

THE VOYAGE OF H.M.S. PANDORA *by Edward Edwards R. N. & George Hamilton, edited by Basil Thomson*—In Pursuit of the Mutineers of the Bounty in the South Seas—1790-1791.

MEDUSA *by J. B. Henry Savigny and Alexander Correard and Charlotte-Adélaïde Dard* —Narrative of a Voyage to Senegal in 1816 & The Sufferings of the Picard Family After the Shipwreck of the Medusa.

THE SEA WAR OF 1812 VOLUME 1 *by A. T. Mahan*—A History of the Maritime Conflict.

THE SEA WAR OF 1812 VOLUME 2 *by A. T. Mahan*—A History of the Maritime Conflict.

WETHERELL OF H. M. S. HUSSAR *by John Wetherell*—The Recollections of an Ordinary Seaman of the Royal Navy During the Napoleonic Wars.

THE NAVAL BRIGADE IN NATAL *by C. R. N. Burne*—With the Guns of H. M. S. Terrible & H. M. S. Tartar during the Boer War 1899-1900.

THE VOYAGE OF H. M. S. BOUNTY *by William Bligh*—The True Story of an 18th Century Voyage of Exploration and Mutiny.

SHIPWRECK! *by William Gilly*—The Royal Navy's Disasters at Sea 1793-1849.

KING'S CUTTERS AND SMUGGLERS: 1700-1855 *by E. Keble Chatterton*—A unique period of maritime history-from the beginning of the eighteenth to the middle of the nineteenth century when British seamen risked all to smuggle valuable goods from wool to tea and spirits from and to the Continent.

CONFEDERATE BLOCKADE RUNNER *by John Wilkinson*—The Personal Recollections of an Officer of the Confederate Navy.

NAVAL BATTLES OF THE NAPOLEONIC WARS *by W. H. Fitchett*—Cape St. Vincent, the Nile, Cadiz, Copenhagen, Trafalgar & Others.

PRISONERS OF THE RED DESERT *by R. S. Gwatkin-Williams*—The Adventures of the Crew of the Tara During the First World War.

U-BOAT WAR 1914-1918 *by James B. Connolly/Karl von Schenk*—Two Contrasting Accounts from Both Sides of the Conflict at Sea D uring the Great War.